Resources
on
Professional Development Schools
An Annotated Bibliography and Resource Guide

Second Edition

ISMAT ABDAL-HAQQ
COMPILER

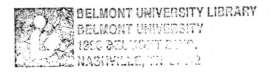

CLINICAL SCHOOLS CLEARINGHOUSE/ADJUNCT ERIC
CLEARINGHOUSE ON CLINICAL SCHOOLS
ERIC CLEARINGHOUSE ON TEACHING AND
TEACHER EDUCATION
AMERICAN ASSOCIATION OF COLLEGES
FOR TEACHER EDUCATION

Preparation of this publication was supported by funds from the AT&T Foundation and the Office of Educational Research and Improvement (OERI), U.S. Department of Education (DOE), under contract number RR93002015. The opinions, conclusions, and recommendations expressed herein do not necessarily reflect the views or opinions of the AT&T Foundation, OERI, DOE, or the American Association of Colleges for Teacher Education (AACTE).

Cite as:

Abdal-Haqq, I., (Comp.). (1997). *Resources on professional development schools: An annotated bibliography and resource guide*. (2nd ed.). Washington: Adjunct ERIC Clearinghouse on Clinical Schools, ERIC Clearinghouse on Teaching and Teacher Education, American Association of Colleges for Teacher Education.

Copies may ordered from:
AACTE Publications
One Dupont Circle NW, Suite 610
Washington, DC 20036-1186
(202) 293-2450
URL: <http://www.aacte.org>
e-mail: iah@aacte.nche.edu
Single copies: $18
Plus $5 shipping & handling

Typesetting, design, and layout by Ismat Abdal-Haqq. Cover design by W.M.Graphics, Washington, DC.

CONTENTS

Introduction

When I started constructing the first edition of this annotated bibliography, *Resources on Professional Development Schools* (Abdal-Haqq, 1993), my chief concern was finding enough sources on professional development schools (PDSs) to justify a publication at all. With this second edition, the primary task has become deciding what to include, given the space and time constraints I face. Although the literature on professional development schools remains modest when compared to some other topics in education, the growth in the number of books, articles, conference papers, and other resources is notable. The 1993 resource guide contained 119 annotations of print material; the present edition contains 153 annotations, only one of which is included in the first edition. A majority of the sources included in this resource guide were published or produced between 1993 and 1997.

The professional development school made its debut as a significant player in the continuing saga of school reform in the mid-1980s when the Holmes Group (1986) used the term in its first report, *Tomorrow's Teachers*. While the focus of this report was preparation and support of teachers and the professionalization of teaching, the authors also articulated a compelling vision of schooling and school change, exemplified by the professional development school.

Education reformers recognized the necessary link between quality education for children and quality preparation of teachers and other school-based educators. Effective professional preparation requires a sound theoretical knowledge base, integrated with coherent, systematic, authentic, and comprehensive practicum experiences. These components come together in the concept of professional development schools.

Theoretically, PDSs provide the exemplary clinical sites needed to give educators-in-training meaningful practical experiences. They are intended to be learner-centered schools where teaching and the learning experiences of children reflect the best available knowledge about educational practice. Preservice educators therefore learn to teach in environments that reflect the best in teaching. As such, PDS are frequently compared to teaching hospitals; they are functioning facilities serving clients, as well as sites that train professionals. Preservice teachers in PDSs are often called interns, and novice teachers in some settings are referred to as residents. In fact, some PDSs conduct "rounds" as part of the preservice field experiences (Neubert, 1997).

Four major purposes comprise the PDS mission: (1) initial preparation of teachers and other school-based educators, (2) professional development of practicing teachers and other school-based educators, (3) exemplary instructional and other educational experiences for students, and (4) applied inquiry designed to improve practice. PDSs are collaborative partnerships. Partners include one or more higher education institutions and one or more schools and/or school districts. Some partnerships include teachers unions or health and human service agencies. Parity among partners is a significant PDS commitment. PDSs are "real world" schools that reflect the demographic and sociocultural environments in which today's and tomorrow's teachers will most likely practice. These schools are committed to equity in policy and practice for all participants.

It is uncertain exactly how many PDSs have been established. Survey and informal data collected by the Clinical Schools Clearinghouse produce an estimate of more than 650 P-12 schools (Abdal-Haqq, 1996). These schools are known by various names—professional practice school, clinical school, professional development center, partner school—and are found in at least 38 states and several foreign countries (Abdal-Haqq, in press). The PDS model for professional development of teachers has been explicitly or tacitly endorsed by several states and national education agencies (Levine, 1996; Macy, Macy, & Kjelgaard, 1996; Maryland Higher Education Commission, 1995; Minnesota State Board of Teaching, 1994).

As enthusiasm for PDSs has grown, the PDS literature has followed suit. Not only has the total number of PDS-related references grown dramatically, we are also seeing more research on PDS effectiveness. Because information on evaluation and assessment has traditionally been rather sparse in the PDS literature, in selecting sources for this resource guide, weight was given to research reports or documents that include information on outcomes, particularly student outcomes. Other selection factors included timeliness—the focus is on recent literature—and the significance of the topic. For example, we have relatively few sources about PDS implementation in foreign countries, so such material is generally included. I have also tried to include material that may not routinely make its way into the mainstream of education literature. These resources include audiovisual material, electronic sources, and fugitive literature. Many annotations in this resource guide are tagged with icons indicating type of resource, such as research report, foreign source, and electronic document, among others.

A majority of the annotated sources have been abstracted for the ERIC database. For each such annotation, an ERIC accession number follows the facts of publication. Availability information is provided for material that is not yet accessible through ERIC or that is unlikely to be. Newsletters, PDS-related videos, electronic resources, and networks and information centers are identified in the appendices.

This annotated bibliography and resource guide has been compiled and published to facilitate location of sources of information on professional development schools. Clinical Schools Clearinghouse staff hope that readers find the guide useful. Comments and feedback on the content and organization are welcome.

References

Abdal-Haqq, I. (Comp.). (1993). *Resources on professional development schools: An annotated bibliography*. Washington, DC: Adjunct ERIC Clearinghouse on Clinical Schools, ERIC Clearinghouse on Teacher Education, American Association of Colleges for Teacher Education. ED359177

Abdal-Haqq, I. (1996). An information provider's perspective on the professional development school movement. *Contemporary Education, 67*(4), 237-240.

Abdal-Haqq, I. (in press). *Professional development schools: Weighing the evidence*. Thousand Oaks, CA: Corwin Press.

Holmes Group. (1986). *Tomorrow's teachers*: *A report of the Holmes Group*. East Lansing, MI: Author. ED270454

Levine, M. (1996). *Professional development school standards. Synthesis paper. A work in progress*. Unpublished manuscript. National Council for the Accreditation of Teacher Education, Profesional Development Schools Standards Project, Washington, DC.

Macy, D. J., Macy, S. J., & Kjelgaard, P. (1996). *CPDT. Centers for Professional Development and Technology. State-wide evaluation study. Final summary report.* Wills Point, TX: Macy Research Associates.

Maryland Higher Education Commission. (1995). *Teacher Education Task Force report.* Baltimore, MD: Author.

Minnesota State Board of Teaching. (1994). *Developing a residency program as part of teacher licensure. A report in accordance with Minnesota statutes.* 1993 Supplement. Section 125.230, SUBD.7.(b). St. Paul, MN: Author. ED381488

Neubert, B. (1997). A professional development academy for the humanities—Towson State University Department of Secondary Education. In R. D. Benton (Ed.) *Partnerships for learning: Real issues and real solutions.* Monograph Series vol. 2, no. 2. Oshkosh, WI: Teacher Education Council of State Colleges and Universities.

Section 1
Annotations A-H

Annotations in this chapter are alphabetized by author. When facts of publication are followed by an EJ or ED number, the resource has been abstracted for the ERIC database. Full-text microfiche copies of most documents (citations followed by an ED number) are available at more than 900 locations nationally, including all ERIC clearinghouses and major university libraries. Ordering information for full-text print copies of most documents can be found in the ERIC database abstract or obtained by contacting the ERIC Document Reproduction Service: 1-800-443-ERIC (443-3742). For information on article reprints, contact ACCESS ERIC: 1-800-LET-ERIC (538-3742).

Throughout this section, PDS is used as the abbreviation for professional development school. Icon key:

  multi-author book or journal theme issue

  electronic document

  non-U.S. source or subject

  research report

1.1 Abdal-Haqq, I. (Comp.). (1993). *Resources on professional development schools: An annotated bibliography.* Washington, DC: Adjunct ERIC Clearinghouse on Clinical Schools, ERIC Clearinghouse on Teacher Education, American Association of Colleges for Teacher Education. ED359177

The 119 annotations and other resources included in this bibliography and resource guide relate to professional development schools, professional practice schools, clinical schools, partner schools, and similar institutions. The print sources deal with a variety of topics: institutionalization, collaboration, definition, resource allocation, development, implementation, and evaluation. Concept papers, research reports, handbooks, bibliographies, course outlines, policy statements, and historical perspectives are represented. The appendices include lists of newsletters that frequently contain information on PDSs, audio cassette tapes of conference sessions, and groups or organizations that are associated with PDSs, as well as a fact sheet on the Clinical Schools Clearinghouse.

1.2   Abdal-Haqq, I. (Comp.). (1995). *Professional development schools: A directory of projects in the United States* (2nd, ed.). Washington, DC: American Association of Colleges for Teacher Education. ED391778

This directory profiles 66 PDS partnerships, which include 78 higher education institutions and 301 individual P-12 schools. A national survey supplied contact information, as well as data on partners, grade level, program features, funding sources, network affiliation, and technology use. The survey data collection form and a bibliography of references on profiled programs are included.

1.3   Abdal-Haqq, I. (1996). *Locating resources on professional development schools*. ERIC Digest 95-3. Washington, DC: ERIC Clearinghouse on Teaching and Teacher Education. ED398216

This digest examines several categories of resources that include PDS-related material. The discussion includes suggestions for more productive ERIC searching, examples of electronic resources, locating fugitive literature, and contact information for several information centers.

1.4   Abdal-Haqq, I. (in press). *Professional development schools: Weighing the evidence.* Thousand Oaks, CA: Corwin Press.

Recent literature related to the four major PDS goals— initial teacher preparation, inservice professional development, student learning, and applied inquiry— is reviewed. Topics include program features, evaluation and outcomes, PDS interface with three reform initiatives—integrated services, technology infusion, and parent involvement—equity, time, and, financing. The review attempts to illuminate what actually goes on in PDSs, how programs deal with thorny issues, the extent to which existing programs fulfill the PDS mission, and the model's potential for bringing about meaningful improvements in schooling, particularly for marginalized and vulnerable groups.

1.5   Abdal-Haqq, I. (in press). *Preparing teachers for urban schools: A report on the Teachers for Tomorrow program.* Washington, DC: American Association of Colleges for Teacher Education.

Activities and outcomes of the AT&T Teachers for Tomorrow (TFT) program are the focus of this publication. The TFT sites established or expanded PDS partnerships in urban settings in five states. The program sought to improve the clinical phase of teacher education to make it more relevant to preparing teachers for urban schools, to reduce the attrition rate of urban teachers, and to improve the learning experiences of students in participating schools.

1.6   Alber, S. (1995, April). *Meeting the challenge for high level parental involvement in an urban professional development school.* Paper presented at the Association of Teacher

Educators Summer Conference, Williamsburg, VA.

This paper focuses on how high-level parent involvement was used to promote equity for parents of students in an elementary Detroit PDS. Beginning with a discussion of theoretical and research considerations related to parent involvement in urban settings, the authors proceed to a description of a project that led to formation of a parent leadership team. Training, activities, problems, and outcomes are discussed.

1.7   American Association of Colleges for Teacher Education. (1995). *RATE VIII: Teaching teachers—Relationships with the world of practice.* Washington, DC: Author. ED379265

Utilizing data collected from a survey of a random sample of the 700-plus member institutions of the American Association of Colleges for Teacher Education, this report focuses on relationships that schools, colleges, and departments of education have with P-12 schools and other education stakeholders. Of the institutions surveyed, 46% had PDS or partner school arrangements with P-12 schools. The report relates attributes of reported partner school relationships.

1.8   Anderson, M., Boles, K., Abascal, J., Barand, M. D., Bourne, L., Brown, J., Cassidy, M. B., & Holzapfel, D. (1995, April). *The reflective mentoring seminar: Providing means for teachers to cross boundaries in a professional development school.* Paper presented at the annual meeting of the American Educational Research Association, San Francisco. ED396996

This paper describes the structure and activities of the Windham Partnership for Teacher Education, a collaborative that includes four rural Vermont elementary PDSs, a high school PDS, and the School for International Training graduate program in foreign language teacher education. The program is characterized by three integrated activities: (1) use by preservice teachers of authentic materials and varied foreign language pedagogical methods to integrate foreign language instruction and multicultural education; (2) one-year classroom internships for MAT students; and (3) professional development for intern mentors.

1.9   Andrews, S. V., & Smith, P. G. (1994, February). *Multiple levels of collaboration in professional development schools: A continuum of professional development.* Paper presented at the annual meeting of the American Association of Colleges for Teacher Education, Chicago. ED374082

This paper discusses a university-public school partnership involving 10 PDSs and Indiana State University. These PDSs contribute to a continuum of professional development for educators at all levels: preservice teachers, inservice teachers, public school administrators, and teacher educators. Professional development schools provide opportunities to redefine roles and relationships between and among preservice teachers, inservice teachers, college faculty, and elementary and secondary students. Three strategies that have made important contributions to successful efforts to implement collaborative professional development at the sites are outlined: engaging in inquiry, building a team spirit, and mutual critique. A collaborative strategy and structure for inquiry is described: a team consisting of preservice teachers, inservice teachers, and college faculty worked together to build the language arts and social studies methods course curriculum in ways that link the elementary school curriculum to the college curriculum. Examples of the following program features and efforts are also outlined: building a team spirit in the college classroom, planning and debriefing time for cooperating teachers and their preservice students; and professor-researchers becoming learners in their own classrooms.

1.10   Arends, R., & Winitzky, N. (1996). Program structures and learning to teach. In F. B. Murray (Ed.), *The teacher educator's handbook: Building a knowledge base for the preparation of teachers* (pp. 526-556). San Francisco: Jossey-Bass. ED394902

The authors maintain that teacher education needs to be reformed and that correcting many of the weaknesses identified by teacher educators, policymakers, and others requires changes in program structures. The chapter explores alternative program structures and analyzes their advantages and disadvantages. Three internal program structures receive attention: time structures, degree structures, and curriculum and activity structures. Professional development schools are discussed as one contemporary reform initiative designed to increase program coherence and address structural issues.

1.11   Ariav, T., & Clinard, L. M. (1996, July). *Does coaching student teachers affect the professional development and teaching of cooperating teachers? A cross-cultural perspective.* Paper presented at the Second International Conference, Mofet Institute, Department of Teacher Education, Ministry of Education, Culture, and Sport, Israel.

In this study, which utilized a collaborative action research approach, the authors examine the perceptions of cooperating teachers who are coaching student teachers in PDSs affiliated with University of California-Irvine and Beit Berl College in Israel. Specifically, the study focuses on the contributions made by teachers to student teacher development, the benefits derived by these teachers, and the effects of coaching on the teaching and professional life of cooperating teachers. Findings within and across sites are related.

1.12   Baker, B. R. (1996). *The role of the professional development school to prepare teachers of young children. A description of two models: The Hillcrest Professional Development School and the LaVega Primary School.* ED394647

This paper describes the development and operation of two professional development schools by the School of Education at Baylor University (TX). These schools were organized to develop and demonstrate: (1) high quality learning programs for diverse students; (2) practical, thought-provoking preparation for novice teachers; (3) new understandings and professional responsibilities for experienced educators; and (4) research projects that add to all educators' knowledge about how to make schools more productive. The Hillcrest PDS and LaVega Primary School were organized along these principles, emphasizing theme-based interdisciplinary teaching, multiaged groups, technology, cooperative learning, inclusion, performance assessment, and outdoor learning environments. Mixed-age groups of 40 students are taught cooperatively by a master teacher, a first-year teacher, and student teachers from the university. An appendix contains lists of procedures, objectives, and teacher evaluation forms used in the PDS program.

1.13 Barba, R., Seideman, I., Schneider, H., & Mera, M. (1993). *School of Education Secondary Teacher Education Program. Professional Development Schools Project. Status report.* Unpublished manuscript. School of Education, University of Massachusetts, Amherst.

Focusing on secondary schools, the PDS partnership between University of Massachusetts-Amherst and four area school districts began in 1986, initiated by the concern of a local principal and acting superintendent with the impending shortage of well-qualified teachers. This report discusses the partnership's history, characteristics, and structure. Profiles of each site are included, as well as summaries and samples of presentations, articles, workshops, grant funding, and publicity related to the project.

1.14 Bell, N. M. (1995). *Professional development sites: Revitalizing preservice education in middle schools.* ED382583

This case study reports on the experiences of teachers and student teachers enrolled at Charleston Southern University (SC) during the process of developing and implementing professional development sites at one urban and two rural middle schools. The study examines the phases of development that teachers go through in the process of developing such sites and how teachers' level of development affects overall school development. It also examines the benefits, to student teachers and to supervising teachers, of PDS-based training of preservice teachers. The focus of PDS activity at the three sites was preservice teacher training. Student teachers at one of the PDSs responded positively to a two-week orientation to the school, designed by a core group of teachers (n=6) at the site, which introduced preservice teachers (n=5) to teaming, the school advisement program, teaching strategies, management techniques, lesson planning, and media. Both student teachers and supervising teachers concurred on three primary benefits of the PDS program: (1) support was available for both preservice and cooperating teachers; (2) student teachers became familiar with the school and its procedures, which gave them a framework for understanding school operations and made the supervising teachers' jobs easier; and (3) student teachers had the chance to observe various teaching styles.

1.15 Benton, P., (Ed.). (1990). *The Oxford Internship Scheme: Integration + partnership in initial teacher education.* London: Calouste Gulbenkian Foundation. ED374086

This book contains essays about a specific and local reform, the Oxford Internship Scheme, which was developed and implemented by a partnership between Oxford University (England) and the local education authority in Oxfordshire. The internship program represents a commitment to the school-based training of teachers and, in some ways, is analogous to the teaching hospital concept. The 12 chapters are: (1) "The Reform of Teacher Education" (Judge); (2) "Ideas and Principles Guiding the Internship Scheme" (McIntyre); (3) "The Process of Change" (Pendry); (4) "The Internship Model" (Benton); (5) "Learning To Teach: Designing and Running Two Curriculum Programmers" (Davies and others); (6) "Being a Teacher: Whole-School Aspects of the Internship Scheme" (Woolnough and others); (7) "The Impact on the Schools" (Hagger); (8) "A Headteacher's Perspective" (Green); (9) "The LEA Engagement" (Brighouse); (10) "An Evolving Course" (Allsop, & Corney); (11) "Internship: A View from Outside" (Hirst); and (12) "Internship: A View from Abroad" (Warren-Little). Two appendices are included: "The Definition of Roles" and "List of Important Abilities." The latter refers to assessment criteria for interns.

1.16   Benton, R. D. (Ed.). (1997). *Partnerships for learning: Real issues and real solutions*. Oshkosh, WI: Teacher Education Council of State Colleges and Universities.

More than 25 case studies, descriptions, and related documents from professional development school and other partnerships among the members of the Teacher Education Council of State Colleges and Universities (TECSCU) are featured in this volume.

1.17   Berkeley, C. (1995). *Professional development schools: An annotated bibliographic resource*. Sacramento, CA: California State University, Institute for Education Reform. ED398172

The 47 references annotated in this bibliography reflect a range of authors, document types, and PDS issues. For the most part, entries are longer and more detailed than typical annotations. Most references have publication dates between 1986 and 1995. The introduction identifies five institutional sources of information on PDSs and briefly outlines the goals and characteristics of PDSs.

1.18   Berry, B., Boles, K., Edens, K., Nissenholtz, A., & Trachtman, R. (1996). *Inquiry and professional development schools*. Unpublished manuscript. National Center for Restructuring Education, Schools, and Teaching, Teachers College, Columbia University, New York.

The focus of this paper is inquiry in and about PDSs. Understandings, findings, and possibilities related to inquiry are summarized. Overall, the authors conclude that knowledge about the nature and results of PDS-related inquiry is sparse at present. They discuss a number of organizational and philosophical constraints that have hampered inquiry efforts thus far. This paper is one of five commissioned by the National Center for Restructuring Education, Schools, and Teaching (NCREST) on aspects of PDS development and implementation [*see:* Murrell & Borunda; Teitel, Reed, & O'Conner]. Anticipated publication date for the collection is fall 1997.

1.19   Boles, K., & Troen, V. (1994, April). *Teacher leadership in a professional development school.* Paper presented at the annual meeting of the American Educational Research Association, New Orleans. ED375103

Findings from a study, which examined the development of leadership skills and roles among teachers in a professional development school, indicate the emergence of a nontraditional teacher leadership paradigm at the PDS. In contrast to typical teacher leadership models, in which carefully selected and screened teachers are placed in leadership positions, the teacher leadership paradigm that has emerged is characterized by a form of collective leadership in which teachers develop expertise reflecting individual interests. The Learning/Teaching Collaborative (L/TC) is a PDS that was initiated in a Brookline (MA) elementary school in 1987 by two teachers to improve the work of teachers, reform preservice teacher education, and mainstream special needs students more effectively. Four components of the L/TC are team teaching, school-university collaboration, special education inclusion, and alternative professional teaching time (APT). APT allows teachers at least one day per week to assume an alternative role (e.g., curriculum writer, researcher, student teacher supervisor, college teacher). The eight teachers who were interviewed for this study indicated that the PDS nurtured teacher leadership, leadership activities grew naturally out of professional interests and working in teams, teaching practices changed significantly, and professional relationships improved. Teachers experienced the greatest growth and development in the following areas: team teaching and collaboration, preservice teacher education, curriculum development, research, and governance.

1.20   Book, C. L. (1996). Professional development schools. In J. Sikula, T. J. Buttery, & E. Guyton (Eds.), *Handbook of research on teacher education*, 2nd edition (pp. 194-210). New York: Simon & Shuster Macmillan.

This chapter reviews research literature on professional development schools. Definitions and research methods used to conduct most PDS research are discussed. Cautions for future research are articulated, and concerns and benefits of research in and about PDSs are related.

1.21   Bright, G. W., & Vacc, N. N. (1994, April). *Changes in undergraduate preservice teachers' beliefs during an elementary teacher certification program.* Paper presented at the annual meeting of the American Educational Research Association, New Orleans. ED375087

This study examined whether inclusion of cognitively guided instruction (CGI) in a mathematics methods course for 34 undergraduate preservice teachers at the University of North Carolina at Greensboro would improve their teaching performance, compared to controls. The Beliefs Survey, with four subscales

(Role of the Learner, Relationship between Skills and Understanding, Sequencing of Topics, and Role of the Teacher) was administered four times. The mathematics methods course occurred between the second and third administrations, and student teaching occurred between the third and fourth administrations. The survey revealed that preservice teachers in both cohorts changed beliefs to a more constructivist orientation to teaching mathematics during their professional program of study. In both cohorts, the greatest change in beliefs occurred during the semester in which the mathematics methods course was taught, suggesting that dealing explicitly with mathematics pedagogy influences preservice teachers' thinking about teaching and learning mathematics. The beliefs of the CGI cohort continued to change fairly dramatically during the student teaching semester while the beliefs of the non-CGI cohort did not. In response to open-ended questions, preservice teachers acknowledged the need for teachers to know what children were thinking. There were few suggestions from either cohort on how CGI should be actualized in instruction. Implications for teacher preparation are offered.

1.22 Bullough, R. V., Jr., Kauchak, D., Crow, N., Hobbs, S., & Stokes, D. (1997). Long-term PDS development in research universities and the clinicalization of teacher education. *Journal of Teacher Education 48*(2): 85-95.

In this article, the authors explore the clinicalization of teacher education, the result of increased use of clinical faculty in the PDSs affiliated with the University of Utah. Presented are a brief history of the PDS program and the staffing patterns that evolved, results of a descriptive case study focusing on the role of clinical faculty, and a discussion of the implications of findings for future PDS development. Financing, university faculty attitudes, and emerging conflicts are among the topics and issues examined.

1.23 Bullough, R. V., Jr., Kauchak, D., Crow, N., Hobbs, S., & Stokes, D. (1997). Professional development schools: Catalysts for teacher and school change. *Teaching and Teacher Education, 13*(2): 153-171.

Data from questionnaires and interviews with teachers and principals form the basis of this discussion of the impact of PDS involvement on teacher professional growth and school change in seven PDS sites that have existed for five or more years. Program results were mixed across sites, affected by context variables such as district support, principal role, school and university faculty stability, student body composition and grade level, school and faculty size, and the nature of teachers' involvement. Implications for PDS program development and research are discussed, and a range of policy issues are explored. The seven sites discussed in the article form part of a partnership between University of Utah-Salt Lake City and two local districts.

1.24   Burke, W. I., & Galassi, J. P. (1997). *The Research Triangle Professional Development Schools Program: One response to the call for university-school education partnerships.* Unpublished manuscript. School of Education, University of North Carolina at Chapel Hill.

PDSs are discussed as a response to the call for university-school education partnerships by the Dean's Council of the University of North Carolina at Chapel Hill Board of Governors. Historical predecessors of PDSs, as well as current PDS developments, are reviewed. PDS concepts and issues are illustrated through a discussion of the Research Triangle Professional Development School, a formal partnership between the university and four local districts. Issues important in planning and implementation are enumerated.

1.25   Cambone, J., Zambone, A., & Suarez, S. C. (1996, April). *Are they learning as we expected them to learn? An evaluation of the preparation of special education teachers using a professional development school model.* Paper presented at the annual meeting of the American Educational Research Association, New York. ED394251

This paper reports initial results from an evaluation of the first two years of implementation of a master's level teacher preparation program at Wheelock College (MA) for teachers of students with special needs (TSSN). An overview of the program notes that the intensive 14-month experience leads to a masters degree in education and standard certification in both elementary and special education. The program is organized around three phases (fundamentals, teaching-to-learn and learning-to-teach, and knowledge integration) and four learning vehicles: (1) coursework; (2) practice (a full-year, full-time internship); (3) mentoring and supervision by both the cooperating teacher and college supervisor; and (4) utilizing prior experiences and self-examination. Evaluation involved extensive data collection (such as employer evaluation surveys and student surveys) during and following the program. Findings are detailed for each of the four learning vehicles. The evaluation concluded that the program design is coherent with the PDS model and students are learning as expected, but that the mentoring and practice components seem less effective than expected.

1.26   Campbell, T. A., Strawderman, C., & Reavis, C. A. (1996). Professional development schools: Collaboration and change. *Teacher Education Quarterly 23*(2), 94. EJ535039

Case study methodology guided collection and portrayal of data on the development and implementation of a professional development school collaborative by Texas Tech University and the Lubbock Independent School District. Discussion of the collaborative's experiences is framed by three phases of the documented change process: initiation, implementation, and continuation. Brief reports of positive outcomes, including student outcomes, are included.

1.27   Castleman, J. B. (1996). *Improving field experiences for rural preservice teachers through the establishment of a professional development school.* Unpublished practicum paper. Nova Southeastern University. ED401067

This practicum report focuses on the creation of a PDS designed to improve field experiences for early childhood education majors at a rural private college. The goal of the project was to increase the number of qualified teachers at a local primary school who would be willing to participate in the supervision of student teachers. The initial step in establishing the PDS was the formation of a steering committee composed of teachers, an administrator, and other school personnel. Program evaluation revealed that most PDS participants were positive about the partnership between the college and the school, participation rates were high for steering committee meetings and functions, there was an increase in the number of teachers willing to supervise students teachers, and student teachers were able to be placed in a quality field experience in close proximity to the college campus. However, a majority of the teachers did not complete a state-recommended course for student-teacher supervisors designed to improve their teaching skills as well as their proficiency as supervisors. The appendix includes teacher survey, evaluation forms, and PDS mission statement and goals.

1.28   Chance, L. H., & Rakes, T. A. (1994, July). *Differentiated evaluation in professional development schools: An alternative paradigm for preservice teacher evaluation.* Paper presented at the CREATE National Evaluation Institute, Gatlinburg, TN. ED376162

The "Practice Teaching Portfolio" is one component of an authentic assessment system for evaluating student teachers that has been implemented in nine professional development schools associated with the University of Memphis. Designed to develop an authentic record of the student teachers' performance, the system combines full lesson observations, related classroom observations, snapshot evaluations, logs, and lesson and unit plans. Contents of the portfolios reflect a differentiated model of evaluation, with contributions from the student teacher, cooperating teacher, and university liaison. Contents include student teacher self-ratings, lesson plans, cooperating teacher evaluative comments, work samples or documents approved by the cooperating teacher, and results of "snapshot evaluations." When conducting a snapshot evaluation, the university liaison uses a structured instrument to observe and note a range of specific classroom behaviors on the part of the student teacher. The differentiated model of student teacher evaluation is a collaborative model in which classroom teachers (cooperating teachers) become equal partners with university liaisons in the supervision of student teachers. This partnership reflects the professional development schools' collaborative approach to other educational activities, including team teaching, joint research, and teacher training.

1.29   Chase, S., Merryfield, M., & Chism, E. (1996, April). *Bridging the gap between campus and school through collaboration in a professional development school network in social studies and global education.* Paper presented at the annual meeting of the American Educational Research Association, New York.

Incorporating the perspectives of a field professor, university professor, and a preservice teacher, this article discusses a school-university collaboration in teacher education in social studies and global education at Ohio State University. Major steps in developing the PDS network, lessons learned, and concerns and issues evolving from the network's experiences since 1991 are related. Tensions and communications problems between and among school and college faculty are highlighted.

1.30   Christenson, M. A., & Serraro, S. (1997). Cooperative learning in a hostile environment. *Teaching and Change, 4*(2), 137-156.

Two PDS teachers describe their efforts to adapt and implement cooperative learning strategies that meet the needs of children in an urban second-grade classroom. The teachers attempted to answer two questions: How can cooperative learning be implemented, in a manner that avoids unnecessary confusion, with second graders who are inexperienced with this format; and what academic and social benefits accrue to economically disadvantaged children when cooperative learning strategies are used?

1.31   Clark, R. W. (1995). *National Network for Educational Renewal: Partner schools.* Seattle: University of Washington, Center for Educational Renewal. ED380418

This guide describes the general expectations and major purposes of partner schools in the National Network for Educational Renewal (NNER). Partnerships between these schools and higher education institutions focus on training teachers and renewing schools. NNER partner schools share a commitment to the 19 postulates enumerated by John Goodlad in *Teachers for Our Nation's Schools.* Through partner schools, schools and universities seek to accomplish four purposes: (1) educate children and youth, (2) prepare educators, (3) provide professional development, and (4) conduct inquiry. For each of these four purposes, the document lists expectations. Under "educating children and youth" the expectations are for a learning community, equity, and excellence. Under "preparing educators," the expectations are for collaboration, pedagogy, curriculum and attitudes, and academic knowledge. Under "providing professional development," the expectations are for collaboration and student-driven needs; linkages between theory, research, and practice; special needs; and interprofessional connections. Under the "inquiry" purpose, the expectations are for critical and social inquiry, reflective practice, and inquiry as scholarship. Finally, for all purposes, the document states that partner schools should be supported by sufficient staff, time, and money. For all the expectations, specific examples are offered.

1.32   Clark, R. W. (1995). *Partner schools*. Seattle, WA: University of Washington, Center for Educational Renewal. ED380417

In this directory, profiles are given of the partner schools included in the 14 sites that make up the National Network for Educational Renewal. These partnerships are committed to simultaneous renewal of schools and teacher education and utilize the 19 Goodlad postulates as their guiding principles.

1.33   Clark, R. W. (1996). *What school leaders can do to help change teacher education* (2nd ed.). AACTE Forum Series. Washington, DC: American Association of Colleges for Teacher Education. ED399221

This booklet proposes four actions that school leaders, particularly school district superintendents, can take to promote simultaneous improvement of educator education and public schools. It is proposed that school leaders: (1) make preservice education a true priority, (2) cooperate in establishing partner schools that serve as professional development schools, (3) make professional development a high priority, and (4) work with various constituents to encourage bold curriculum and instruction innovations in preservice education and professional development. Particular steps may include collaborating with parents, administrators, teachers, community members, and higher education institutions to set policies and goals related to school district involvement in educating educators; actively participating in recruiting and selecting students for preservice teacher education; enrolling preservice students in cohorts and assuring that minority students are included in the cohorts; supporting substantive school-college collaboration; developing support among parents, unions, and policy-making bodies, such as school boards and legislatures; allocating funds and other resources to assist in improving the education of educators; creating centers of inquiry; and helping university faculty and administrators understand school culture. The recommendations included in this booklet were drawn, in part, from conversations with superintendents from some of the 16 settings in the National Network for Educational Renewal and from other districts.

1.34   Clark, R. W. (1997). *Professional development schools: Policy and financing. A guide for policymakers*. Washington, DC: American Association of Colleges for Teacher Education.

Utilizing data collected from several of the National Network for Educational Renewal sites, as well as other sources, the author constructs two basic cost models for PDS financing, provides estimates of start-up and operating costs, and summarizes typical financing schemes. The document outlines the benefits to schools and colleges of PDS programs and suggests approaches to partnership financing.

1.35   Clemson-Ingram, R. L., & Fessler, R. (1997). The Maryland Redesign of Teacher Education: A commitment to system reform. *Action in Teacher Education, 19*(1), 1-15.

In this article, the authors trace the national teacher education reform movement and make explicit connections between elements of that reform and statewide reform in Maryland, as explicated in the Maryland Redesign of Teacher Education. Extended preservice internships in PDS settings are an integral component of the Maryland Redesign. PDS implementation at Johns Hopkins University and the statewide Professional Development School Consortium are briefly described.

1.36 Colburn, A. (1993). *Creating professional development schools*. Fastback 352. Bloomington, IN: Phi Delta Kappa Educational Foundation. ED359146

Several factors may interfere with effective collaboration between universities and K-12 schools, a key element in the process of establishing and operating professional development schools (PDSs). These factors relate to differences in school and university cultures and the impact of these differences on the respective faculties. Among the differences are those in work tempo, professional focus, career reward structure, sense of personal power and efficacy, academic freedom, and approach to preservice teacher education. Investigation of four professional development school sites reveals a variety of strategies that schools and universities (Virginia Commonwealth University, Kansas State University, Michigan State University, and the University of Northern Colorado) are using to overcome barriers to collaboration. This booklet provides a rationale for professional development schools, lists common characteristics, briefly describes examples of successful operations, places PDSs in historical context, identifies factors that contribute to successful collaboration, and suggests things that school administrators can do to achieve successful collaboration.

1.37 Collinson, V., Hohenbrink, J., Sherrill, J., & Bible, R. (1994). *Changing contexts for changing roles: Teachers as learners and leaders in universities, professional development schools, and school districts*. Paper presented at the annual conference of the Association for Supervision and Curriculum Development, Chicago. ED374091

This paper synthesizes the results of three case studies that focus on urban and suburban elementary teachers who are engaged in new roles: as learners, as clinical educators, and as leaders. Results of the studies suggest that epistemological issues, workplace contexts, and an ethic of care, which is especially noticeable in collegial relationships, have considerable impact on teachers as leaders and learners. The first case study examined interactions among the school- and university-based faculty who, for two terms, were co-teachers of a social studies methods course. The second study investigated teachers in the role of clinical educators; i.e., school-based teacher educators who are involved in teacher preparation, beginning teacher support, teacher development, and school and college professional development, as well as maintaining a significant classroom role. The study investigated factors that affect teachers functioning as clinical educators in a professional development school and a university setting. The third case study investigated six veteran teachers, recognized by their colleagues as leaders, and identified attributes shared by these teachers. Among the issues that emerged from the case studies are: the isolation sometimes experienced by teachers who step outside their traditional roles, the importance of personal support for these teachers, and the manner in which differences between university and school culture influence the ways teachers function in new roles.

1.38　　Cook, S. A., & McClean, B. (1995). The professional development school in Canada. *McGill Journal of Education, 30*(3), 311-321. EJ522293

　　　　The authors describe a cooperative venture between a Canadian university and a high school. A university professor taught two units of a social studies class and shared her impressions, thoughts, and suggestions with school staff. Findings from the undertaking, as well as interactions with school staff and subsequent developments, are discussed.

1.39　　Crow, N., Stokes, D., Kauchak, D., Hobbs, S., & Bullough, R. V., Jr. (1996, April). *Masters cooperative program: An alternative model of teacher development in PDS sites.* Paper presented at the annual meeting of the American Educational Research Association, New York. ED399223

　　　　Findings are reported from a study that investigated the influence of a two-year cooperative masters of education program, based at University of Utah-Salt Lake City, as a vehicle for professional development and school renewal. Semistructured interviews and questionnaires were used to collect data from 25 experienced teachers based in three secondary and two elementary professional development schools (PDSs). The dominant theme to emerge from the data was the impact of the cooperative program on teachers as sustained change agents. This theme played itself out in four major areas of participants' lives: teachers' beliefs and roles, the classroom, the school, and the development of a community of learners. There was a continuous emphasis on inquiry throughout the program, during which teachers conducted year-long research projects. Respondents linked their practice of sustained inquiry to increases in confidence levels, role changes, and increased activism. A majority of respondents indicated that (a) the program changed their teaching practices, (b) change continued after they completed the program, and (c) these changes were also linked to the experience of conducting an action research inquiry project. The program also stimulated teachers to give more choice and voice to their own students. While individual action research projects and other aspects of the program positively impacted some schools and influenced school change efforts at several sites, some teachers reported little or no school change. The program's contribution to developing a community of learners at various sites is also discussed.

1.40   Darling-Hammond, L. (Ed.). (1994). *Professional develop-ment schools: Schools for developing a profession.* New York: Teachers College Press. ED364996

Contents: "Developing Professional Development Schools: Early Lessons, Challenge, and Promise" (Darling-Hammond); "Wells Junior High School: Evolution of a Professional Develop-ment School" (Miller & Silvernail); "In Pursuit of a Dual Agenda: Creating a Middle Level Professional Development School" (Grossman); "Permission, Persistence, and Resistance: Linking High School Restructuring with Teacher Education Reform" (Whitford); Perils and Potentials: A Tale of Two Professional Development Schools" (Snyder); "Professional Development in Action: An Idea with Visiting Rights" (Lythcott & Schwartz); "The Los Angelas Professional Practice School: A Study of Mutual Impact" (Lemlech, Hertzog-Foliart, & Hackl); "Creating Profes-sional Development Schools: Policy and Practice in South Carolina's PDS Initiatives" (Berry & Catoe); and "Change for Collaboration and Collaboration for Change: Transforming Teach-ing Through School-University Partnerships" (Robinson & Dar-ling-Hammond).

1.41   Darling-Hammond, L., Bullmaster, M., & Cobb, V. L. (1995). Rethinking teacher leadership through professional devel-opment schools. *Elementary School Journal, 96*(1), 87-105. EJ510580

In this article, the authors trace possibilities for new forms of teacher leadership that are emerging in PDSs. Data are examined from in-depth case studies of seven PDSs, and these data are supplemented by research from several other PDSs. The analysis produces three claims: teacher leadership is inextricably connected to teacher learning; teacher leadership can be embedded in tasks and roles that do not create artificial, imposed, formal hierarchies; and such approaches may lead to a norm of expanded teacher roles, with resulting improvement in the capacity of schools to respond to student needs.

1.42   Deer, C. E., & Williams, D. (1995). *Professional develop-ment schools: Do they have anything to offer to teacher education in Australia?* ED399218

This paper traces the origins of professional development schools (PDSs), describes their characteristics, examines a network of PDSs, considers the place of PDSs in developing the teaching profession, addresses problems and concerns associated with developing and sustaining PDSs, and draws implications for teacher preparation and the teaching profession in Australia. Estab-lishing a statewide network of professional development schools has been a major objective of the Michigan Partnership for a New Education; however, this paper identifies several obstacles that are likely to impede the program's progress towards its ultimate goals. Brief descriptions of three PDS-related resource centers are pro-vided. Three major problems and concerns are identified: (1) the cost, in time and money; (2) the insufficient number of PDSs; and (3) the status of PDSs as an alternate, rather than mainstream, route to becoming a teacher. The authors conclude that the PDS is a promising approach to restructuring and improving both schools and faculties of education in Australia.

1.43   DeWert, M. H., & Cory, S. L. (1996). Becoming partners: Building a school/university collaboration focused on teaching and learning with technology. *Journal of Computing in Teacher Education, 2*(3), 8-12. EJ528680

Collaborative grant conceptualization and writing gave depth to a school-university partnership that applied for and secured a grant to enhance, through technology, the environmental education program of a local elementary school. The proposal development process is described and critically analyzed. Lessons learned about collaborative planning and its impact on subsequent implementation are shared, and mutual benefits are outlined. University of North Carolina-Chapel Hill is one of the partners.

1.44   Duffy, G. G. (1994). Professional development schools and the disempowerment of teachers and professors. *Phi Delta Kappan, 75*(8), 596-600. EJ481328

Although professional development schools are vehicles for reform, getting them "online" can overshadow the spirit of collaborative egalitarianism essential for success. One solution is to involve teachers and professors in resolving an immediate professional problem associated with school improvement or teacher preparation. The decision to become a professional development school can then be made by knowledgeable, experienced teachers.

1.45   Duquette, C., & Cook, S. A. (1994). Five Ontario professional development schools. *Journal of Professional Studies, 1*(2): 60-72. EJ523830

This article reports findings from a study of five Canadian PDSs and analyzes strengths, weaknesses, and barriers to success from the perspectives of student teachers, associate (cooperating) teachers, and university faculty. School administrator support, communication between partners, and financial resources are among the factors related to PDS success that are discussed.

1.46   Educational Partnerships. [Theme issue]. (1994). *National Association of Laboratory Schools Journal*, *19*(1).

The seven articles in this theme issue cover a range of topics related to educational partnerships, including history of the partnership movement, current trends, and philosophical issues. Each article includes discussion of a specific PDS, partner school, or laboratory school site or project. Two of the articles focus on similarities and differences between laboratory schools and PDSs.

1.47   Forrest, L., Putnam, J., Narusis, E. M., & Peeke, P. (1993). *Win/win restructuring: Counseling psychology collaboration with teacher education in professional development schools.* ED370889

Integration of counseling psychology and teacher education characterizes the PDS model described in this paper. The approach generates recommendations for restructuring schools, colleges, and departments of education (SCDEs). Because the involvement of counseling psychologists in PDSs has created a win/win situation from the perspective of teacher education and counseling psychology faculty, as well as the school-based PDS personnel, a more thorough examination of this collaboration may provide insights from actual practice in restructuring to guide reform activities in SCDEs. After setting the enterprise in a historical context, the paper summarizes data from interviews with principals, teachers, teacher educators, and counseling psychologists who are actively collaborating in PDSs. The lessons learned from these collaborations are identified and used to create recommendations for SCDE reform.

1.48   Fountain, C. A., & Evans, D. B. (1994). Beyond shared rhetoric: A collaborative change model for integrating preservice and inservice urban educational delivery systems. *Journal of Teacher Education, 45*(3), 218-27. EJ494041

This article describes a change model that links urban public school and teacher preparation renewal. The model evolved from a three-year school district-university collaboration in Jacksonville, Florida. Topics include the professional development continuum, from early field experiences to professional educator experiences, school- and university-based clinical faculty, and institutionalization of program features.

1.49   Fullan, M. (1995). Contexts: Overview and framework. In M. J. O'Hair & S. Odell (Eds.), *Educating teachers for leadership and change. Teacher education yearbook III,* (p.1-10). Thousand Oaks, CA: Corwin Press.

The author discusses the limitations of existing efforts to improve teacher development as a strategy for reform and improving student learning. PDSs, identified as one example of university-school partnerships, are one of the efforts discussed. Regarding their effectiveness in bringing about substantive change in teacher development and school reform, the author concludes that "rhetoric outstrips reality" (p. 3). A more comprehensive framework for teacher development than commonly exists is proposed, and the six interrelated domains that make up the framework are discussed.

1.50   Gardner, W. E., & Libde, A. A. (1995). Professional development schools: How well do they travel? *Journal of Education for Teaching, 21*(7), 303-316.

To implement successfully in the United Arab Emirates the generally accepted principles of operation for professional development schools (PDSs), pragmatic modifications are needed to four major aspects of PDSs: the decision-making process, the need to build autonomous institutions, equity and reciprocity between school and university, and the preferred classroom teaching methodology.

1.51   Garland, K. (1995). The information search process: A study of elements associated with meaningful research tasks. *School Library Media Annual (SLMA), 13,* 171-183. EJ516594

This study investigated research projects at a secondary PDS to determine successful task factors. Results show that student choice of topic, group work, relationship to course content, clear communication by teachers of goals and evaluation methods, and process instruction influenced student satisfaction. The article includes instruments used in the study.

1.52   Gottesman, B., Graham, P., & Nogy, C. (1993). *South Carolina Center for the Advancement of Teaching and School Leadership: Professional development schools.* Rock Hill: South Carolina Center for the Advancement of Teaching and School Leadership, Winthrop College. ED366549

In 1990, the South Carolina Center for the Advancement of Teaching and School Leadership was established by the state's legislature to provide support to schools undergoing or planning restructuring. The center assists schools to analyze needs, establish goals, and implement those goals. Technical assistance and college and school faculty training are among the center's tasks. The center established a restructuring network, which includes the 28 approved teacher education programs in South Carolina and more than 100 associate schools throughout the state. These schools, which become partner schools and professional development schools, have pivotal roles in driving educational change in the center's model for school improvement. In addition, the center is a partner in the South Carolina collaborative chosen as one of the eight Goodlad sites engaged in developing model programs that link school restructuring to teacher education reform. Five colleges and universities are partners in the collaborative: Benedict, Furman, Columbia, University of South Carolina, and Winthrop. This paper describes elements of the school-college partnership at each of these institutions, focusing on noteworthy features such as an innovative approach to college faculty load at a professional development school affiliated with the University of South Carolina, partner school criteria, and recruitment of males and persons of color for rural and neighborhood schools. The paper presents 17 guidelines for establishing statewide collaboratives to facilitate school restructuring.

1.53   Grau, I. IV. (1996, January). *Teacher development in technology instruction: Does computer coursework transfer into actual teaching practice?* Paper presented at the annual meeting of the Southwest Educational Research Association, Dallas, TX. ED394949

This study examined the technology preparation component of two University of Houston-Clear Lake (UHCL)

preservice teacher education programs: the traditional teacher education program and the Teacher Education Advancing Academic Achievement Model (TEAM) collaborative teacher education program. Some characteristics of TEAM were: a year-long, site-based internship; university and site-based mentor teams; professional development of public school teachers and university faculty; higher education and public school collaboration in professional development schools; and infusion of technology into the public school and education curriculums. The traditional program and TEAM were compared by measuring the extent to which graduates transferred their newly acquired computer-technology skills and knowledge into their first-year of actual teaching practice. Responses to a technology use questionnaire indicated that a greater mean percentage of the 15 first-year TEAM graduates: (1) acquired greater knowledge of the functions and features of computer software and hardware, (2) learned how to use a variety of computer software and hardware tools to enhance their performance, and (3) developed skills and knowledge necessary to integrate computer software and hardware with instruction when compared to 15 traditional UHCL education graduates. Six recommendations to help preservice and inservice programs, school districts, and local schools ensure commitment to the long-term use of computer software and hardware are suggested.

1.54 Gross, S., (Ed.). (1993). *Constructing teaching and research practice in elementary school mathematics.* Elementary Subjects Center Series No. 92. East Lansing: Michigan State University, Center for the Learning and Teaching of Elementary Subjects, Institute for Research on Teaching. ED364405

This report contains case studies of two teachers who attempt to go beyond traditional mathematics curriculum and instruction. There are important differences in the contexts of teaching and in the approaches to studying teaching and learning in these two classrooms. The first case study describes a teacher who draws upon professional experiences to initiate change in the classroom. The authors describe elements of the teacher's mathematics teaching, using Curriculum and Evaluation Standards of the National Council of Teachers of Mathematics (NCTM) as a framework for analysis, then analyze the teacher's views about instructional issues, focusing on connections between beliefs and practice. The second case study describes a teacher involved in a mathematics study group in a PDS. The authors chronicle the changes in this teacher's thinking and practice during a three-year period, focusing on her views about, and understanding of, mathematical content, the nature and role of discourse about mathematics, and what constitutes evidence of mathematical learning. In discussing the kinds of changes these teachers made, the authors also explore the role of collaboration among teachers and between teachers and university participants

1.55 Hargreaves, A., & Jacka, N. (1995). Induction or seduction? Postmodern patterns of preparing teachers to teach. *Peabody Journal of Education, 70*(3), 41-63. EJ514185

This article considers moral, emotional, and political influences on teachers' emerging identities. The authors analyze how one beginning teacher acquired and sustained innovative instructional methods, recommend training in varied instructional methods, contest the use of PDSs, and suggest changes in the cultures and contexts of beginning teachers' education.

1.56 Harris, R. C., & Harris, M. F. (1993). Partner schools: Places to solve teacher preparation problems. *Action in Teacher Education, 14*(4), 1-8. EJ482514

Problems and solutions associated with a five-year university-school collaboration to implement partner schools are outlined. A sample of findings from research and external evaluation is given as preliminary evidence of the partner school concept's feasibility.

1.57 Hausfather, S. J., Outlaw, M. E., & Strehle, E. L. (1996). Relationships as a foundation: Emerging field experiences within multiple college-school partnerships. In T. Warren (Ed.), *Partnerships in teacher education* (pp. 27-41). Lanham, MD: University Press of America.

The authors describe restructuring of education courses and field experiences at Berry College (GA), a small liberal arts college, and the resulting impact on relationships within the college of education and PDS classrooms. While preliminary analysis reveals benefits to teacher education students as a result of closer supervision and more intense field experiences, little movement appears to have been made toward larger school reform goals.

1.58 Hayes, H. A., & Wetherwill, K. S. (1996, April). *A new vision for schools, supervision, and teacher education: The professional development system and Model Clinical Teaching Project.* Paper presented at the annual meeting of the American Educational Research Association, New York. ED400229

This paper discusses a reform project (The Professional Development System: Collaboration for Quality Education) collaboratively developed by the University of North Carolina at Wilmington and the Brunswick and Duplin County (NC) public school systems. The project takes a systems approach to changing the way teachers are educated and draws upon theoretical frameworks from the areas of organizational reform, adult learning, professional development of educators, and clinical supervision. Four goals guide program design and implementation: (1) to improve public school classrooms; (2) to improve teacher education, particularly student teaching and field-based components of methods courses; (3) to improve school/school system and school of education practices; and (4) to change the student teaching supervision model to learner-centered supervision. Program activity is centered in elementary clinical sites. Narrative statements from program graduates, classroom teachers, public school administrators, field-based teacher educators, and university faculty supply glimpses of program operations. Findings related to the impact on schools, teachers, preservice teachers, and teacher education programs are presented, and implications of the results are discussed. The professional development system incorporates formative and summative evaluation strategies, including interviews and a follow-up study of graduates that considered employability, licensure, and assessment of program graduates by employing principals. In general, results suggest that the program is working.

1.59   Hecht, J. B., Bland, S. J., Schoon, P. L., & Boschert, K. (1996). *Professional development school 1995-96. A research report.* Normal: Illinois State University, College of Education, Technological Innovations in Educational Research Laboratory.

Presented are results from a study designed to gauge the effect of the PDS program at Illinois State University (ISU) on participating teacher education students, ISU faculty, and district teachers. PDS participants were compared to traditional program participants utilizing a 150-item questionnaire covering eight different areas of teaching and teacher preparation and an open-ended survey, which included several more general questions. The report discusses several statistically significant differences between the two groups that suggest that the PDS effort has had a positive influence on the perceptions of both teacher education students and mentor teachers, as well as producing satisfaction with students and the program on the part of ISU faculty. Critical issues related to program continuation and stability are also discussed.

1.60   Higgins, K., & Merickel, M. L. (1997). The promise and the promises: Partnerships from a university perspective. *Teacher Educator, 32*(3), 165-184.

This study describes issues related to the genesis of two university-middle school partnerships as experienced and related by university faculty members involved in the process. Both benefits and tensions arising from the partnerships are discussed. Although such partnerships have considerable potential for changing teacher education, several constraints, including the university's reward system, hamper implementation efforts.

1.61   Hill, N., & Lauter, N. (1996). *Professional development school partnership. Progress review: School year 1995-1996.* New York: Teachers College, Columbia University.

This report reviews various initiatives launched by a partnership between Teachers College, a local school district, and a local teachers union. Included are discussions of the professional development academy partnership history, continuing initiatives, professional development activities, preservice preparation, rewards and incentives, governance, goals and objectives, and future initiatives.

1.62   Hoffman, N. E., Reed, W. M., & Rosenbluth, G. S. (Eds.). (1997). *Lessons from restructuring experiences: Stories of change in professional development schools.* Albany: State University of New York Press.

The chapters in this volume focus on the experiences of

PDSs in the Benedum Collaborative in West Virginia: "The Nature of Professionalism in the Context of School Reform" (Dempsey); "Collaboration Between K-12 Schools and Universities" (Shive); "The Benedum Collaborative: The Story of an Educational Reform Effort" (Steel & Hoffman); "The Story of Two Changing Teachers" (Steel, Jenkins, & Colebank); "The Story of Two Principals: Constructing Leadership, Balancing Tensions, and Creating Relationships" (Dempsey, Hart, & Lynch); "The Story of Changing Practices: Classroom Based Collaboration as a Model for a Communications Program" (Borsch, Oaks, & Prichard); "The Story of a Changing Program: West Virginia's First Science, Math, and Technology Center" (Gaston, Francis, Crescenzi, & Phillips); "The Story of a Changing School" (Field & Barksdale-Ladd); "The Story of Changing School-University Relationships" (Hoffman, Rosenbluth, & McCory); "Teachers' Perspectives on School Change: Lessons from the Classroom" (Saab, Steel, & Shive); "Reconsidering Assessment to Be Reflective of School Reform" (Webb-Dempsey); "Impact on Colleges of Education" (Hawthorne).

1.63　Holmes Group. (1995). *Tomorrow's schools of education.* East Lansing, MI: Author. ED399220

　　This report contains nine chapters: "A New Beginning"; "The Heart of the Matter: Three Kinds of Development"; "Special Knowledge for Educators"; "Participating in Policy Development"; "Commitment to Diversity"; "Human Resources: Making People Matter"; "The Core of Learning: What All Educators Must Know"; "The Professional Development School: Integral to Tomorrow's School of Education"; and "New Commitments and New Kinds of Accountability for the TSE." To correct the problem of uneven quality in the education and screening of educators for U.S. schools, the report proposes an altered mission for schools of education. Knowledge development, professional development, and policy development lie at the heart of the mission. To fulfill this mission, Holmes Group member institutions are challenged to raise their quality standards and make important changes in curriculum, faculty, location of work, and student body. Among the challenges are the following: the education school's curriculum should focus on the learning needs of the young and development of educators at various stages of their careers; university faculties should include teachers, practitioners, and other individuals who are at home working in public schools; programs that prepare school personnel and teacher educators need to actively recruit, retain, and graduate a more ethnically diverse student body; faculty and students in schools of education should work predominantly in professional development schools rather than on college campuses; and education schools should join together to form an interconnecting set of networks at local, state, regional, and national levels to ensure better work and accountability.

1.64   Hopkins, W. S., Hoffman, S. Q., & Moss, V. D. (1997). Professional development schools and preservice teacher stress. *Action in Teacher Education, 18*(4), 36-46.

The authors describe a research project that compared the changes in stress scores of preservice teachers in a pilot PDS with scores of preservice teachers in a traditional teacher preparation program. Statistically significant increases in stress occurred during the culminating field experience for the PDS preservice teachers. The authors suggest that total immersion in intense PDS field experiences may require a different type of support system for the preservice teacher and caution against assuming that these teachers will automatically develop adequate stress-coping abilities without such support.

1.65   Houston, W. R., Clay, D., Hollis, L. Y., Ligons, C., Roff, L., & Lopez, N. (1995). *Strength Through Diversity: Houston Consortium for Professional Development and Technology Centers.* Houston, TX: University of Houston, College of Education.

This report includes three documents: (1) *Strength Through Diversity: Houston Consortium for Professional Development and Technology Centers*, which gives background on the consortium, provides an overview of program goals and features, and presents outcomes for both school and university teacher education students; (2) a 1996 conference paper, presented to the Association of Teacher Educators when the consortium received the association's annual distinguished teacher education award; and (3) a set of profiles of the consortium's 16 PDSs. Positive results on state-mandated teacher licensure exams and student achievement tests support belief in the efficacy of the program's approach to preservice education and professional development. Technology infusion, performance assessment, and school and university faculty development activities are described. Descriptive statistics related to program outcomes and characteristics are included, as well as benchmarks and other details about the program's implementation strategy. The consortium includes nine partners—five school districts and regional service centers and four universities—in the Houston area.

Annotations in this chapter are alphabetized by author. When facts of publication are followed by an EJ or ED number, the resource has been abstracted for the ERIC database. Full-text microfiche copies of most documents (citations followed by an ED number) are available at more than 900 locations nationally, including all ERIC clearinghouses and major university libraries. Ordering information for full-text print copies of most documents and many journal articles can be found in the ERIC database abstract or obtained by contacting the ERIC Document Reproduction Service: 1-800-443-ERIC (443-3742). For information on article reprints, contact ACCESS ERIC: 1-800-LET-ERIC (538-3742).

Throughout this section, PDS is used as the abbreviation for professional development school. Icon key:

multi-author book or journal theme issue

electronic document

non-U.S. source or subject

research report

2.1   Implementing the agenda of simultaneously renewing schools and the education of educators: National Network for Educational Renewal. (1995). [Special issue]. *Record in Educational Leadership, 15*(2).

Nineteen articles, including an introduction by John Goodlad, are included in this issue. Organized in three sections—"Some Critical Issues," "Implementing the Postulates—Putting the Necessary Conditions in Place," and "Resources"—

the features focus on the work of partnerships in the National Network for Educational Renewal (NNER). The resources section includes a directory of NNER settings, a list of the 19 Goodlad postulates, and a discussion of references related to the NNER and other PDSs.

2.2 Ishler, R., & Edens, K. (1995). *Professional development schools: What are they? What are the issues and challenges? How are they funded? How should they be evaluated?* Kingston, RI: Association of Colleges and Schools of Education in State Universities and Land Grant Colleges and Affiliated Private Universities.

Findings from the work of the Task Force on Professional Development Schools, appointed by the leadership of the Association of Colleges and Schools of Education in State Universities and Land Grant Colleges and Affiliated Private Universities, are reported in this collection of essays. Chapters: "Understanding Professional Development Schools"; "Professional Development Schools and Interprofessional Collaboration"; "Funding Sources for Professional Development Schools"; " Financial Issues and Professional Development Schools"; "Funding Professional Development Schools: Opportunities for Federal Support"; "Dilemmas, Barriers, and Challenges to Sustaining Professional Development Schools"; "Evaluating Professional Development Schools"; and "Promoting Professional Development Schools." Two appendices include criteria for funding PDSs by the Texas Education Agency and the South Carolina Commission on Higher Education.

2.3 Jennings, N., Peasley, K., & Rosaen, C. (1997). Learning with experience. In S. Feiman-Nemser & C. Rosaen (Eds.), *Guiding teacher learning* (pp. 89-112). Washington, DC: American Association of Colleges for Teacher Education.

Employing two different guided practice formats, a university researcher worked with two teachers in a professional development school. The first format focused on a weekly seminar in which the researcher and a group of teachers discussed instructional issues and problems. The second format featured the researcher and a classroom teacher coteaching fifth-grade language arts. The complexities of each format are explored, and the potential of each for supporting teachers' learning is examined.

2.4 Johnston, M. (1994). Postmodern considerations of school/university collaboration. *Teaching Education, 6*(2), 99-106. EJ517076

The author discusses problems encountered in a collaborative preservice program and examines differences between the norms and practices of schools and universities from the perspectives of the postmodern theories of deconstruction and feminism.

2.5 Judge, H., Carriedo, R., & Johnson, S. M. (1995). *Professional development schools and MSU. The report of the 1995 review.* (Available online: http://35.8.168.203/kiosk/PDS_Rpt.html; also Professional Development Schools, 513 Erickson Hall, East Lansing, MI 48824)

The authors report findings from their review of the nine PDSs in which Michigan State University is a participating partner, as well as other aspects of the university's involvement with the Michigan Partnership. The report describes the principal benefits derived by various partners in the PDS initiative, including several positive benefits related to student outcomes. Also discussed are constraints and strains that have marked the history of the PDS initiative, background to the initiative, the balance between benefits and problems, and recommendations for future action. The report concludes that both the university and the public would suffer from the demise of the university's involvement in PDSs, a likely occurrence if problems are not adequately addressed. A key factor in shaping future policies is the collective will of the faculty. [*See also Professional Development Schools: Publications and Presentations,* which presents collateral material for this report.]

2.6 King, A. R., Jr., & Mizoue, Y. (1993). A case for university-based professional development and experimental schools: Japanese and American perspectives. *Peabody Journal of Education, 68*(3), 67-79. EJ490241

After brief histories of laboratory schools and comparable Japanese "attached schools," this article promotes preservation of university-controlled schools in a cooperating schools network that provides teacher training and experimentation sites. Although university-controlled schools may have professional development school characteristics, different tasks for specialized cooperating schools are advocated.

2.7 King, N. R. (1996). Opening a professional development school: Do children notice? *School Community Journal, 6*(1), 29-37. EJ527468

Results are reported from a survey of teachers and elementary students after one year of PDS implementation. Results indicate that teachers' enthusiasm for the program did not appear to have spread to students.

2.8 Kjelgaard, P. A., & Norris, C. A. (1994). Teacher training in the professional development model: Implications for students at risk. *Computing Teacher, 21*(7), 12-14. EJ483709

At-risk students are the focus of this article, which highlights professional development schools, restructuring teacher training programs, and integrating modern technology. Topics discussed include university-school collaboration that uses fieldwork to integrate theory and practice, telecommunication networks, distance learning labs, and integrated learning systems and multimedia.

2.9 Kleinsasser, A. M., & Paradis, E. E. (1997). Changing teacher education in the context of a school-university partnership: Disrupting temporal organizational arrangements. *Teacher Education Quarterly, 24*(2), 63-73.

The authors discuss changes in temporal arrangements—i.e., the time spent in interaction in a teacher education program; including student, teacher, professor, and partnership school learning time—within the partnership between University of Wyoming and its 16 partner schools. Interactive compressed video is employed in the program to deliver some graduate-level courses and conduct some meetings.

2.10   Kyle, R. M. J. (1993). *Transforming our schools: Lessons from the Jefferson County Public Schools/Gheens Professional Development Academy, 1983-1991*. Louisville, KY: Gheens Foundation, Jefferson County Public Schools. ED358176

A school-community partnership in Louisville (KY), the Jefferson County Public Schools/Gheens Professional Development Academy, is described. This report provides a framework for assessing Jefferson County School System reforms, carried out over the past eight years, designed to enhance student success in learning. A Spiral of Assessment, in which four sets of indicators were combined in the following ways, was used to evaluate student success and school role: (1) resource indicators reflect major inputs into the educational process, (2) "kaizen" indicators (continuing incremental improvement) reflect continuing growth, (3) milestone indicators reflect progress of students at various intermediate points, and (4) commencement indicators measure outcomes of a cohort of students on completion of their education. The Jefferson County experience is compared with other programs. Schools are transformed through the dynamic interaction among five essential resources that must be mobilized in communities seeking educational improvement: partnerships, leadership, systemic change, development activities, and time. Lessons learned from these interactions include: (1) partnerships involve businesses, community organizations, labor organizations in schools, community, and parents; (2) leadership is requisite in the school system and does not reside in a single office or person; (3) systemic changes require various points of intervention; (4) professional development of teachers and administrators can catalyze innovations and continuing incremental improvements; and (5) changes require time. Systemic, long-term approaches can make a difference, where short-term marginal interventions fail.

2.11   Labaree, D. F. (1995). Disabling vision: Rhetoric and reality in *Tomorrow's Schools of Education. Teachers College Record, 97*(2), 166-205. EJ523874

The author criticizes the Holmes Group's third report, *Tomorrow's Schools of Education*, as counterproductive and contradictory. He suggests that it presents an anti-intellectual vision of schools of education, which, if implemented, would radically narrow the broad range of instructional and intellectual functions of schools of education.

2.12   Lawson, H. A. (1996). Expanding the Goodlad agenda: Interprofessional education and community collaboration in service of vulnerable children, youth, and families. *Holistic Education Review, 9*(1), 20-34.

Current conceptualizations of school-college partnerships,

as exemplified in the partner schools of the National Network for Educational Renewal (NNER), generally are inadequate to meet the needs of vulnerable children and families. The author offers four ways to advance the Goodlad/NNER agenda to incorporate and accommodate work on behalf of vulnerable children and families: extend the moral dimensions of teaching and schooling to all of the helping professions, implement "second generation" partnerships that feature interprofessional collaboration among education and human services agencies, expand the center of pedagogy concept so that it incorporates families and health and human service agencies and their related college departments, and amend the postulates to reflect greater interprofessional practice and community collaboration.

2.13   LeCompe, K., Irby, B. J., & Lara-Alecio, R. (1995). *Community learning: A field-based education model.* ED399222

This paper describes aspects of a program at Sammons Elementary School (Houston, TX) designed to create a learning community that includes preservice teacher education students, practicing teachers, university faculty, and Sammons students and parents. The school has been designated as an Urban Professional Development Site for the Sam Houston State University Center for Professional Development (SHCPD). The site receives federal Title VII Transitional Bilingual Education funds. These funds help to support the community education focus of the program, which includes a major effort to engage parents of linguistically diverse students in encouraging and supporting their children's learning environment. University and school personnel collaborate on two major goals: improving student performance and preparing preservice students for authentic teaching. The paper includes an overview of several elements of the preservice program: curriculum, technology-based activities, field experience, bilingual and multicultural education. The Saturday School at Sammons (SSS), a 10-week Saturday program for parents and children, is the central component of the overall program's parent support services. Parents receive English as a Second Language classes and computer training. In addition to Sam Houston University, Texas A&M University is a partner in SSS, and preservice teachers and university professors from both institutions plan and prepare SSS lessons.

2.14   Levine, M. (1996). Educating teachers for restructured schools. In F. B. Murray (Ed.), *The teacher educator's handbook: Building a knowledge base for the preparation of teachers* (pp. 620-647). San Francisco: Jossey-Bass.

After briefly describing the vision of schooling that is embedded in the education reform movement of the 1990s, the implications of this vision for teacher education are discussed. Professional development schools, or professional practice schools (PPSs), are one element of redesigned teacher education programs that reflect new visions of schooling. The author defines PPSs, addresses what new and practicing teachers need to learn in order work effectively in these schools, identifies some related strategies being developed in PPSs, and discusses relevant issues and policy questions.

2.15　　Levine, M. (1996). *Professional development school standards. Synthesis paper. A work in progress.* Unpublished manuscript. National Council for the Accreditation of Teacher Education (NCATE), Professional Development School Standards Project, Washington, DC.

　　This paper provides an update on the work of the Professional Development School Standards Project, which was initiated in 1995 by NCATE. The paper outlines design principles for PDS standards; summarizes the two kinds of draft standards that have emerged from the project's work—threshold conditions and standards for quality review. How the draft standards might be used is discussed, and indicators for each of four quality standards are provided.

2.16　　Levine, M., & Trachtman, R. (Eds.), *Making professional development schools work: Politics, practices, and policy.* New York: Teachers College Press.

　　Contents: "Learning to Teach in Professional Development Schools" (Zeichner & Miller); "Making It Happen: Creating a Subculture of Mentoring in a Professional Development School" (Beasley, Corbin, Feiman-Nemser, and Shank); "How the Emergence of Teacher Leadership Helped Build a Professional Development School" (Boles & Troen); "Reinventing Leadership in Professional Development Schools" (Trachtman & Levine); "The Idea of the University in an Age of School Reform: The Shaping Force of Professional Development Schools" (Lyons, Stroble, & Fischetti); "The Organization and Governance of Professional Development Schools" (Teitel); "Professional Development Schools: Their Costs and Financing" (Clark & Plecki); "Worthy of the Name: Standards for Professional Development Schools" (Sykes); "The Stories of Insiders" (Trachtman); "The Thomas Paine Professional Development Schools" (King); The Thomas Jefferson Professional Development School" (Lancy);" The Oak Street Professional Development School" (Snyder & Goldman).

2.17　　Long, J. (1995, February). *Research analysis of professional development school graduates and traditional phase I and phase II graduates.* Paper presented at the annual meeting of the Association of Teacher Educators, Detroit. ED382570

　　Elementary education majors at Emporia State University (ESU) (KS) were subjects in a research project designed to administer, analyze, and interpret a variety of quantitative and qualitative measures of two groups. An experimental group consisted of 16 interns placed at one of two professional development schools that ESU operates in partnership with local school districts. A control group consisted of 16 student teachers who completed the traditional teacher preparation model at ESU. Results indicated: (1) there were no significant differences in National Teacher Examination scores between PDS interns and student teachers in the control group; (2) no major significant difference was found between the two groups' responses to the Teacher Education Questionnaire, which measures beliefs about teaching, learning, and subject matter; (3) the experimental (PDS) group was significantly more positive toward inclusion of children with disabilities in mainstream classrooms; and (4) PDS graduates were better prepared for the first year of teaching than graduates from traditional student teaching experiences. The appendices include: statistical summaries of findings; "Attitudes Toward Mainstreaming Survey, ESU Adaptation"; a summary of professional development school outcomes, which focuses on competencies of PDS graduates; "Intern Feedback on the PDS Program re: Preparation for Teaching"; and "Sample Questions from the Teacher Education Questionnaire."

2.18   Lyons, N. (1996). A grassroots experiment in performance assessment. *Educational Leadership, 53*(6), 64-67. EJ519782

Teaching portfolios are a critical component of overall assessment of preservice teachers in the University of Southern Maine's Extended Teacher Education Program. An intensive, one-year internship occurs in PDSs linked to five school districts that participate in the Southern Maine Partnership.

2.19   Macy, D. J., Macy, S. J., & Kjelgaard, P. (1996). *CPDT. Centers for Professional Development and Technology. Statewide evaluation study. Final summary report.* Wills Point, TX: Macy Research Associates.

Results are reported from an evaluative study of 21 Centers for Professional Development and Technology (CPDTs) funded by the Texas legislature over a four-year period, 1992-93 through 1995-96. Included among the CPDTs are 35 universities, 113 school districts, and 412 PDSs. The purpose of the study was to gather evaluative data related to the progress and contributions of the centers toward the goals of systematic change in teacher preparation and student learning. Major findings related to CPDT graduate performance, student outcomes, redesign of teacher preparation, institutionalization, professional development outcomes, level of collaboration, financial support, minority recruitment, and technology infusion are reported.

2.20   Masaaki, H. (1993). Clinical education and the role of attached schools in preservice teacher education. *Peabody Journal of Education, 68*(3), 53-57. EJ490239

The "attached schools" of national universities in Japan are comparable to U.S. laboratory schools. This article discusses the history of attached schools, their present condition, and restructuring the role of these schools to make them clinical schools, compatible with overall reform of clinical education for beginning teachers.

2.21   Martin, D. (1996). *Project Achieve. 24 month progress report.* Unpublished manuscript, Department of Education,

Gallaudet University, Washington, DC.

Project Achieve is a collaborative activity involving Gallaudet University's deaf education teacher preparation program and five partner schools serving deaf and hard of hearing learners. The PDS model provides the framework for project activities and approaches. A major focus is recruitment and preparation of new teachers from underrepresented groups (i.e., deaf and/or ethnic minority individuals).

2.22 Maryland Higher Education Commission. (1995). *Teacher Education Task Force report*. Baltimore, MD: Author.

Proposed in this report is the redesign of teacher education in Maryland to reflect a systemic approach to improving teaching and learning in schools. Principles undergirding the proposed comprehensive approach to school improvement are presented. The report includes a framework for defining appropriate preservice and inservice preparation, admission to a PDS, monitoring and assessment, clinical internships, and support for novice and experienced teachers. Also considered are implications of the redesign for approving teacher education programs, implementation, and funding.

2.23 Mattson, B. (1994). *Inservice education and professional development. NSTEP topical bibliography*. Alexandria, VA: National Association of State Directors of Special Education. ED377647

This bibliography on inservice education and professional development in special education lists 364 references grouped into the following categories: general references (82); adult learning (7); needs assessment (12); planning and designing staff development (11); incentives (1); models of inservice and continuing education (33); mentoring programs (6); professional development schools (3); evaluation (10); team orientation (14); school improvement and restructuring (16); integration and inclusion (33); administration (6); secondary level (4); beginning teachers (6); early childhood education (15); teacher focused (27); paraprofessionals (16); technology and distance learning (40); and papers from the Technology in Teacher Education fifth annual conference of the Society for Technology and Teacher Education (22). References date from 1980 through 1994 and include journal articles, books, conference papers, and government reports.

2.24 Mayes, I. J. (Ed.). (n.d.). *Teaching tips. A booklet of ideas for the experienced and inexperienced teacher*. Loveland, CO: Thompson Valley High School.

This handbook is given to all preservice and beginning teachers at Thompson Valley High School, a PDS partner of Colorado State University-Fort Collins. The booklet offers practical guidelines for a range of instructional and noninstructional tasks and situations, as well as time management strategies, and interpersonal relations. Staff members contributed to the guide, which was edited by the school-based PDS coordinator.

2.25   McDaniel, E. (1993). Computers and school reform. *Educational Technology, Research and Development, 41*(1), 73-78. EJ462811

Computers can be used to help school reform by shifting the emphasis from information transmission to information processing. Highlights include creating learning communities that extend beyond the classroom, educationally oriented computer networks, professional development schools for curriculum development, and new methods of student evaluation.

2.26   McDevitt, M. A. (1996). A virtual view: Classroom observation at a distance. *Journal of Teacher Education, 47*(3), 191-195.

The author describes a technology-mediated early field experience, which incorporates an emerging PDS network and a two-way television system. Technology is used to provide more opportunities for preservice students to observe exemplary teaching, as well as to facilitate meaningful dialogue with teachers and other students. Analysis of qualitative and quantitative data on 49 elementary teacher certification candidates suggests that technology-mediated observations, linked with in-person observations, can stimulate enthusiasm in preservice and inservice teachers about the possibilities for improving schooling through educational technology.

2.27   Metcalf-Turner, P. (1994, November). *School-university collaborations: An examination of faculty perceptions and attitudes.* Paper presented at the annual meeting of the Mid-South Educational Research Association, Nashville, TN. ED389250

This study investigated faculty perceptions and attitudes toward organizational change in colleges and schools of education with regard to building collaborative partnerships with public school professionals. The purpose of the study was to confirm the existence of and describe the collaboration formation process within the conceptual framework of PDSs. An inquiry-based, qualitative research design was employed. The basic unit of analysis was the college of education. Seven research institutions were chosen, using purposeful sampling. Sixty-two individual interviews were conducted with selected deans, faculty members, teachers, and relevant stakeholders. A prescribed set of open-ended questions was used to conduct the interviews. Specifically, questions focused on the structural, process, and political dimensions of creating collaborative relationships. Results of the study revealed that there is a clearly defined process that is virtually identical across all seven institutions of higher education involved in establishing PDSs. Collaboration as a process appeared to involve several distinguishable phases of development, namely: formalization and conceptualization, centralization in terms of who governs what, when, and how; and implementation of a mutually agreed upon event to initiate the collaboration process. Equally important were the issues of administrative support and politics, which were perceived to be influential in the collaboration formation process.

2.28 Metcalf-Turner, P., & Fischetti, J. (1996). Professional development schools: Practices, problems and responsibilities. *Metropolitan Universities: An International Forum, 6*(4), 123-138.

The experiences of teacher educators and K-12 practitioners affiliated with the University of Louisville (KY) form the basis of a critical analysis of planning and implementation of collaborative PDS partnerships. Similar undertakings in other locales are included in the analysis.

2.29 Michigan State University. (1995, May). *Professional development schools.* (Program transcript, Michigan Gateways No. 307, first aired May 5, 1995). (Available online: http://web.msu.edu/comptech/gateways/307trn.html; also Michigan Gateways, 212 Communication Arts, Michigan State University, East Lansing, MI 48824-1212; e-mail: MichGate@msu.edu)

PDS teachers and university faculty are interviewed for Michigan Gateways, a television program for math and science teachers. The relation of the PDS to math and science reform is the focus of the program. Other topics include prospects for institutionalization, dissemination, and impact. The transcript includes a resource review that features publications by and about educators in professional development schools. In addition to online access, a transcript and videocassette of this program are available.

2.30 Miller, L., & O'Shea, C. (1994). *Partnership: Getting broader, getting deeper.* NCREST reprint series. New York: National Center for Restructuring Education, Schools, and Teaching, Teachers College, Columbia University.

Experiences in the Southern Maine Partnership are used to frame a discussion of the tension between depth and breadth in partnership implementation. The authors identify some of the issues related to the nature of partnerships as organizations and as vehicles for collaboration and change.

2.31 Million, S. K., & Vare, J. W. (1995). *The collaborative school: Creating a hybrid culture in a professional development school.* Paper presented at the Biennial International Convocation of Kappa Delta Pi, Birmingham, AL. ED395895

Experience with PDS development at Winthrop University (SC) suggests three guidelines for forestalling or ameliorating culture conflict and culture shock: (1) tiers of involvement may help to foster authentic collaboration; (2) providing time and rewards for inquiry nurtures participation by school and university partners; and (3) both parties, at the outset of the venture, should identify self-interests, mutual benefits, and joint goals. School and university faculty in the PDS spend about half of their school day teaching and the balance engaged in reflection, research, and teaching in the teacher education program.

2.32   Minnesota State Board of Teaching. (1994). *Developing a residency program as part of teacher licensure. A report in accordance with Minnesota statutes*. 1993 Supplement. Section 125.230, SUBD. 7.(b). St. Paul, MN: Author. ED381488

In 1993, the Minnesota state legislature established a Teacher Residency Program, and it directed the Minnesota Board of Teaching to report to the education committees of the legislature on developing a residency program as part of teacher licensure. The residency program proposed in this report is one of three components of a restructured teacher licensure program, which includes teacher preparation in an approved teacher education institution, supervised residency in a professional development school, and multiple assessments of teaching knowledge and skills. The one-year residency is a transition for the beginning teacher who has completed preservice preparation but is not yet licensed to teach without supervision. The residency will differ from current beginning teacher programs in several ways. This report addresses a number of issues related to implementation of a residency program, including finance, equity, curriculum, employment issues, ratio of residents to professional development schools , and impact on teachers licensed in other states. A timeline is proposed, which projects full implementation of the restructured licensure system by 2001. In addition to historical background on the residency program, the report includes two appendices: "Minnesota Statutes 1993 Supplement" and "Recommendations of Internship Task Force to Minnesota Board of Teaching Regarding Standards for Internship Programs."

2.33   Moore, K. D., & Looper, S. (1997). Teacher preparation: A collaborative model. *Teacher Educator, 32*(3), 152-164.

This article describes an innovative competency curriculum model for elementary teacher preparation developed at East Central University (OK). The professional development school is the core component of the model. Results of a perceptions survey and workplace competencies measure administered to preservice students and mentors/administrators reveal that program goals are being attained, and there is an overall positive attitude toward the program.

2.34   Morris, V. G., & Taylor, I. (1995). *Parent efficacy, teacher efficacy, and parent involvement in professional development schools. Research report for Frayser Elementary School*. Memphis, TN: University of Memphis, College of Education, Center for Research in Educational Policy. ED399219

The purpose of this study was to examine the relationship between parent efficacy, teacher efficacy, and parental involvement in selected school activities at Frayser Elementary School, a PDS in Memphis (TN), and to present those results in the context of data from eight other schools. Questionnaires and interviews were used to solicit information from Frayser's principal, teachers, and 100 randomly selected parents. Parents and teachers agreed that parental participation in volunteer work at school, telephone calls with teachers, and teacher-parent conferences was low. However, Frayser parents, unlike teachers, reported high levels of parental involvement in helping with homework and spending time on other educational activities. Examination of data from all 9 schools (n=221 parents and 196 teachers) participating in the study revealed that neither parent self-efficacy nor parents' perceptions of teacher efficacy were significantly correlated with parent involvement. However, two demographic variables—family structure and family income—seemed to be moderately and consistently related to parents' and teachers' perceptions of teacher efficacy, parent efficacy, and parental involvement. Teacher self-efficacy scores were significantly and negatively correlated with several indicators of parent involvement. Results suggested a weak negative relationship between teacher self-efficacy and parental involvement and a weak positive relationship between teacher perceptions of parent efficacy and parental involvement. Summaries of data from surveys and copies of the questionnaires are attached.

2.35 Morris, V. G., & Nunnery, J. A. (1993). *Teacher empowerment in a professional development school collaborative: Pilot assessment* (Technical Report 931101). Memphis, TN: Memphis State University, Center for Research in Educational Policy, College of Education. ED368678

The Memphis State University (TN) professional development school (PDS) model was designed to enhance teacher empowerment along certain dimensions cited in the literature: mentoring self-efficacy, teaching self-efficacy, professional knowledge, and collegiality. This PDS model contains three components: supervision of practice teachers, school improvement planning, and clinical professor training. A modified version of the "Teacher Empowerment Inventory" was administered to 140 of the 190 teachers in six elementary schools participating in the PDS program in 1992-1993. Data analysis indicated that teachers in the PDSs felt that the PDS experience enhanced their sense of empowerment by increasing mentoring self-efficacy (degree to which teachers feel able to influence training and entry into the profession of new teachers); teaching self-efficacy (feeling of professionalism, status, and self-esteem as teachers); collegiality (extent of teachers' belief that they work with and influence their peers to improve teaching and learning in their schools); and professional knowledge (teachers' perceptions of their own content knowledge and pedagogical skills). Although teachers perceived themselves to be more empowered along these four dimensions, findings also indicated that these teachers felt that they had very limited power to make changes that might positively affect teaching and learning within their own schools. Included in this paper is an appendix, which contains scale items and reliability estimates.

2.36 Morrison, H. B. (1994, November). *Reflections on the moral content of the professional community vs. moral demands of the community: Focus on Sockett's moral base for teacher professionalism.* Paper presented at the annual meeting of the American

Educational Studies Conference, Chapel Hill, NC. ED378175

This paper describes the moral role of the education profession, discusses the virtuous educator, and examines H. Sockett's concept of "in loco parentis" for the educator and, implicitly, the education profession. Sockett holds that teachers must work as ambassadors for public education in promoting the school's mission and concern for children. The teaching profession has been weakened by social trends, legal decisions, and lack of community support. As an antidote to such weakness, Sockett proposes introducing PDSs where university and local school faculty fashion a microcosm of the united profession. He identifies five elements that exemplify professional virtue: honesty, courage, care, fairness, and practical wisdom. Society's moral vacuum, created by collapse of the family and disappearance of childhood, engenders a need for the virtuous educator. The essential moral nature of the profession demands a return to an "in loco parentis" paradigm, but this paper argues that certain domains are the sole province of parents.

2.37 Morse, S., Daniels, T., & Flieg, F. (1995, February). *An early childhood professional development school: Triumphs and troubles*. Paper presented at the annual meeting of the American Association of Colleges for Teacher Education, Washington, DC. ED382565

This paper presents a case study of a collaboration between the St. Louis Public Schools and Maryville University (MO) to develop an early childhood magnet center and PDS, the Wilkinson Early Childhood Magnet School. This school serves a diverse population of children from age three through second grade. The purpose of the magnet school/PDS is to provide an exemplary education for students and their families, to function as a center for inservice and preservice teacher development, and to inquire into curriculum and practice appropriate for children in the school's age range. Strategies to develop exemplary practice have focused on developing and implementing a constructivist curriculum. Successes that have been achieved can be attributed largely to the sense of shared ownership among school and university staff. Obstacles to implementation have come from a variety of sources, including resistance to the constructivist approach from teachers and conflict between the constructivist curriculum and assessment framework and the requirements and policies of the school district. Shared decision making has produced both ownership, and thus support, of the program, as well as strains on personal relationships and staff schedules. Communication has been the greatest challenge to the collaboration. Although efforts are being made to advance institutionalization of the PDS concept, obstacles from the state, district, university, and school must be overcome.

2.38 Murphy, C. (1996). *The professional development school: Linking the university and the public school. Action research project.* ED400226

Utilizing a consensus decision-making strategy, teachers and an administrator from Parkway Central Middle School

(PCMS) (MO) selected a two-part mission: (1) to establish an atmosphere where students demonstrate respect for themselves, their peers, and all adults; and (2) to evaluate, revise, develop, and implement a new discipline plan that would be more proactive than reactive. To achieve the mission, the Responsibility and Respect Plan was implemented during 1993-1994. Proactive activities, disciplinary management techniques designed to foster responsibility and respect, and new programs were added to existing disciplinary programs. Certain program elements were facilitated by PCMS's professional development school collaborative agreement with University of Missouri-Saint Louis. Data collected on six disciplinary indicators indicated an overall decrease in the number of students involved in disciplinary actions from 1993-1994 to 1994-1995. Findings from surveys of students, teachers, and administrators indicated that respondents considered the Responsibility and Respect Plan's proactive approach and the consensus process effective. Recommendations for improvement in the plan are noted. Two survey questionnaires are included.

2.39   Murrell, P. C., Jr., & Borunda, M. (1997). *The cultural and community politics of educational equity: Towards a new framework of professional development schools*. Unpublished manuscript, National Center for Restructuring Education, Schools, and Teaching, Teachers College, Columbia University.

The authors question whether equity issues can be adequately addressed within the prevailing PDS framework. Thus far, the PDS movement has not been successful in ameliorating inequities in the learning environments of children in public schools, nor has the movement clearly articulated an equity agenda. These failures are in part due to narrow, apolitical conceptualizations of equity. The authors outline nine features of an equity-minded PDS partnership, and these features are used as the basis of recommendations for reformulating an equity agenda. This is one of five papers expected to be published as a collection by NCREST in fall 1997. [See also Berry, et al. and Teitel, Reed, and O'Conner.]

2.40   Myers, C. B. (1996, April). *Beyond the PDS: Schools as professional learning communities. A proposal based on an analysis of PDS efforts of the 1990s*. Paper presented at the annual meeting of the American Educational Research Association, New York. ED400227

A general analysis of professional development school efforts indicates that, overall, the partnerships that were studied devote significantly less attention to ideas about the nature of schools, learning, teaching, the knowledge base for teaching, and teacher learning and professional development than they devote to establishing university-school arrangements, the mechanics of the operation, and the interpersonal relationships involved in bringing university teacher educators and preK-12 teachers together. New teacher induction appears to be the focus of most PDS efforts, but this induction is compromised by insufficient attention to altering the context in which student teachers and beginning teachers learn to teach. The paper suggests that PDS goals should be focused more directly and intensely on improving student and teacher learning. Efforts to reach these goals should be driven by four visions: (1) schools as morally based communities of learners, (2) learning as experience-based intellectual construction, (3) teaching as professional problem solving, and (4) professional knowledge as the knowledge of practice. In addition, PDS efforts should be connected as much as possible to compatible reform proposals and recent thinking about knowledge construction, professional development, and adult learning.

2.41   Myers, C. B. (1996, April). *University-school collaborations: A need to reconceptualize schools as professional learning communities instead of partnerships.* Paper presented at the annual meeting of the American Educational Research Association, New York. ED400228

An analysis of school-university collaborative efforts to establish partnerships and professional development schools (PDSs) suggests that most of these efforts focus on the induction of student teachers, interns, and beginning teachers. Little attention is devoted to helping university-based teacher educators or experienced school faculty study their own practice, improve their work, or reform what they do. Nor is there much attention to rethinking or recreating schools as organizations, reconceptualizing student learning, or adding to the knowledge base for teaching. To a large extent, the partnerships that were studied perpetuated several ideas about schools, learning, teaching, and professional development that have been challenged by many education scholars and reformers. Among these limiting conceptualizations are the view of teaching as a nontheoretically based craft and of schools as factories. Although current reform, restructuring, and partnership endeavors will not, for the most part, create the kinds of schools, learning, teaching, and teacher knowledge and competence that are needed, these efforts can identify: (1) points of intrusion into practice; (2) places of departure from current practice to more meaningful visions of what schools, learning, and teaching should be; and (3) vehicles for reaching these visions. PDSs and comparable broad-scale reform efforts are appropriate starting places for creating learning community schools.

Section 3
Annotations N-Z

Annotations in this chapter are alphabetized by author. When facts of publication are followed by an EJ or ED number, the resource has been abstracted for the ERIC database. Full-text microfiche copies of most documents (citations followed by an ED number) are available at more than 900 locations nationally, including all ERIC clearinghouses and major university libraries. Ordering information for full-text print copies of most documents and many journal articles can be found in the ERIC database abstract or obtained by contacting the ERIC Document Reproduction Service: 1-800-443-ERIC (443-3742). For information on article reprints, contact ACCESS ERIC: 1-800-LET-ERIC (538-3742).

Throughout this section, PDS is used as the abbreviation for professional development school. Icon key:

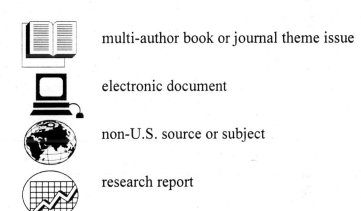

multi-author book or journal theme issue

electronic document

non-U.S. source or subject

research report

3.1   Newman, C., Moss, B., Naher-Snoeden, J., Hruschak, L., Kovack, J., & Pangas, C. (1996, October). *Transforming teacher education, teaching and student learning in a professional development school collaborative: A work in progress.* Paper presented at the annual meeting of the Midwestern Educational Research Association, Chicago.
    Goals 2000 funds supported collaborative redesign of the University of Akron preservice education program, practicing teacher roles, and student learning experiences within a PDS framework. Technology integration is a major component. This paper describes the program and discusses some of the lessons learned.

3.2   Osguthorpe, R. T. (1996, April). *Collaborative evaluation in school-university partnerships.* Paper presented at the annual meeting of the American Educational Research Association, New York. ED398223

A model for developing a partner school and a model for creating a center of pedagogy are presented in this paper. Both are based upon Goodlad principles for school-university partnerships and work by the Brigham Young University-Public School Partnership (BYU-PSP). The author discusses issues related to evaluation of school-university partnerships and describes evaluation activities within the BYU-PSP and other National Network for Educational Renewal sites.

3.3 Osguthorpe, R. T., Harris, R. C., Harris, M. F., & Black, S. (Eds.). (1995). *Partner schools: Centers for educational renewal*. San Francisco: Jossey-Bass. ED382569

National Network for Educational Renewal (NNER) sites are the focus of this volume: "Introduction: Understanding School-University Partnerships" (Osguthorpe, Harris, Black, Cutler, & Harris); "Improving Student Learning" (Kimball, Swap, LaRosa, & Howick); "Strengthening Teacher Education" (Barnhart, Cole, Hansell, Mathies, Smith, & Black); "Promoting Professional Development" (Pines, Michel, & Michelli); "Supporting Collaborative Inquiry" (Hunkins, Wiseman, & Williams); "Launching and Sustaining a Partner School" (Harris & Harris); "Initiating District-Wide Change" (Beglau & Granger); "Promoting Statewide Collaboration" (Little-Gottesman, Nogy, & Graham); "Building Links with Families and Communities" (Lawson, Flora, Lloyd, Briar, Ziegler, & Kettlewell); "Evaluating Partner Schools" (Clark); "Conclusion: The Promise of Partner Schools" (Osguthorpe, Harris, Black, & Harris).

3.4 Papoulia-Tzelepi, P. (1993). Teaching practice curriculum in teacher education: A proposed outline. *European Journal of Teacher Education, 16*(2), 147-62. EJ492147

This article proposes a Greek elementary teacher education curriculum that includes a four-semester, four-level practicum component. The overall program objective is preparation of reflective teachers through interweaving theory and practice in the curriculum. International trends in practicums, clinical schools, and use of technology-rich pedagogical laboratories are discussed.

3.5 Paul, J. (1996). The transformation of teacher education and special education: Work in progress. *Remedial and Special Education, 17*(5), 310-322. EJ530738

The University of South Florida's Department of Special Education has restructured all aspects of its teacher education program in order to respond to educational reforms in institutions of higher education and services integration. Emphasis is on coordination with the local community on specific programs including collaboration with professional development schools.

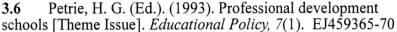

3.6   Petrie, H. G. (Ed.). (1993). Professional development schools [Theme Issue]. *Educational Policy, 7*(1). EJ459365-70

This theme issue contains six articles, including explications of the PDS mission, a case study, and a consideration of administrator preparation. Each of these articles appears in a later, expanded collection of essays edited by Petrie (1995).

3.7   Petrie, H. G. (Ed.). (1995). *Professionalization, partnership, and power: Building professional development schools.* Albany: State University of New York Press.

Contents: "Introduction" (Petrie); "School-University Partnership and Partner Schools" (Goodland); "Design Principles and Criteria for Professional Development Schools" (Murray); "The Professional Development School: Building Bridges Between Cultures" (Stoddart); "The Dialectics of Creating Professional Development Schools: Reflections on Work in Progress" (Henderson & Hawthorne); "Listening But Not Hearing: Patterns of Communication in an Urban School-University Partnership" (Collins); "Why Do Schools Cooperate with University-based Reforms? The Case of Professional Development Schools" (Labaree); "Cultural Transformation in an Urban Professional Development Center: Policy Implications for School-University Collaboration" (Case, Norlander, & Reagan); "Professional Development Schools: A New Generation of School-University Partnerships" (Stallings, Wiseman, & Knight); "Creating a Common Ground: The Facilitator's Role in Initiating School-University Partnerships" (Collay); "Tradition and Authority in Teacher Education Reform" (Ellsworth & Albers); "Professional Development Schools in the Inner City: Policy Implications for School-University Collaboration" (Sewell, Shapiro, Duccette, & Sanford); "Critically Reflective Inquiry and Administrator Preparation: Problems and Possibilities" (Stevenson); "The State Role in Jump-Starting School-University Collaboration: A Case Study" (Teitel); "The Professional Development School: Tomorrow's School or Today's Fantasy" (Creek); "Professional Development Schools: Restructuring Teacher Education Programs and Hierarchies" (Wilder); "Transforming the Discourse: Gender Equity and Professional Development Schools" (Burstyn); "A New Paradigm for Practical Research" (Petrie).

3.8   Policy Studies Associates. (1996). *Learning to collaborate: Lessons from school-college partnerships in the Excellence in Education Program.* Washington, DC: Author.

This report relates lessons learned about project design, implementation, and evaluation from the work of 26 projects supported by the John S. and James L. Knight Foundation's Excellence in Education program. Profiles and summaries of the projects are given. Included among the projects are PDS programs at Gallaudet University and University of North Dakota.

3.9   Powell, J. H., & McGowan, T. M. (1995). Adjusting the focus: Teachers' roles and responsibilities in a school-university collaborative. *Teacher Educator, 31*(1), 1-22. EJ523844

This study investigated whether 12 PDS teachers changed

their perceptions of roles and responsibilities and adjusted their performances to meet this redefinition as a result of participation in an elementary school-university collaborative. Findings suggest that teachers created and maintained three roles: teacher-as-learner, teacher-as-collaborator, and teacher-as-social activist.

3.10 Powell, J. H., & McGowan, T. M. (1996). In search of autonomy: Teachers' aspirations and expectations from a school-university collaborative. *Teaching and Teacher Education, 12*(3), 249-260. EJ530175

Faculty members at an elementary school in its first year as a PDS completed interviews and classroom observations examining how their expectations and aspirations for their role developed over time. Results highlighted five assertions, most of which related to faculty members' degree of control over environment and professional growth.

3.11 *The professional development community: A model for interdisciplinary teaching, service and research to promote student success through wellness for urban children and families.* (1994, May). Unpublished project description. (Available from Center for Collaborative Advancement of the Teaching Profession, School of Education, University of Louisville, Louisville, KY 40292.)

The Wellness Project represents an interprofessional approach to the well-being of children—an approach that attempts to provide a coordinated network of school-based or school-linked educational, health, and social services to children and families. Various components of the project are based at PDSs affiliated with University of Louisville.

3.12 *Professional development school programs in serious emotional disturbance at Marshall Road Center and Pathways/ Hyattsville.* (n.d.). Unpublished project description. (Available from Department of Teacher Preparation and Special Education, The George Washington University, Washington, DC)

This document provides an overview of the professional development school program affiliated with the Department of Teacher Preparation and Special Education at George Washington University. These PDSs provide interdisciplinanry clinical training sites for special educators preparing to work with children who have emotional or behavioral disorders. Interns participate in one-year, full-time intensive internships, during which they work in teams of two with a training teacher. Interns also interact with professionals from the disciplines of social work, psychology, psychiatry, and other related services and allied mental health fields. Program mission, training goals, typical course of study, and history are outlined.

3.13 Professional development schools. [Theme issue]. (1993). *Contemporary Education, 64*(4). EJ485704-17

Fourteen articles comprise this theme issue. Program descriptions, case studies, research reports, and concept papers are included.

3.14 *Professional development schools: Publications and pre-sentations. Collateral evidence in support of the report of the 1995 review*. (1996, March). Unpublished manuscript. (Available from Michigan PDS Consortium, 116D Erickson Hall, Michigan State University, East Lansing, MI 48823.)

More than 500 titles are listed in this document. Most entries include title; authors; and the PDS site that served as the subject, research and development site, or school base for the author. These titles were collected as part of documentation efforts associated with a 1995 review of the nine PDSs affiliated with Michigan State University. [*See* Judge, Carriedo, & Johnson.]

3.15 Professional development schools revisted. [Theme issue]. (1996). *Contemporary Education, 67*(4).

This theme issue contains 15 articles grouped in four sections: "The Promise and Purpose of Professional Development Schools," "Deepening Relationships Through PDS Brings Change in Practice," "Reflection: What We Have Learned," and "Aspects of Evaluation of PDS."

3.16 Putnam, J., Peeke, P., & Narusis, E. M. (1993). *Rethinking educational reform: The inclusion of counseling psychologists on the professional development school (PDS) leadership teams in the PDS schools*. ED370892

Counseling psychologists have a place on PDS leadership teams at local schools working with universities to train teachers and improve schools. They can help team members create healthy relationships, function more effectively, and develop a healthy educational environment. Two critical functions that counseling psychologists can perform in a PDS are remediation (i.e., problem resolution) and development. Semistructured, open-ended inter-views were conducted with administrators, teachers, graduate students, and teacher educators who worked in PDSs. These inter-views were designed to capture perceptions of the actual and potential role of counseling psychologists in PDSs in three areas: remediation, prevention, and development. Examples of remediation activities that were cited include changing negative sterotyping, easing anxiety generated by change, and intervening in dysfunctional professional relationships. Responses from interviewees indicated that a valuable developmental function of counseling psychologists was the counselors' ability to model, facilitate, and promote better communication. The preventive function is demonstrated when counseling psychologists' explore, in advance, such issues as shifts in power and participatory deci-sion making so that PDS faculty are more prepared to understand and function in an evolving school environment.

3.17 Rafferty, C. D. (1995, February). *Impact and challenges of multi-site collaborative inquiry initiatives. Professional develop-ment schools: Changing the work of the school of education*. Paper presented at the annual meeting of the American Association of Colleges for Teacher Education, Washington, DC. ED381489

This paper describes the process of initiating collaborative inquiry projects at Indiana State University's (ISU) 10 PDSs. It discusses what was learned and charts future directions and projected activities. ISU's Collaborative Inquiry Committee/ Team (CIC) established a three-phase collaborative inquiry action plan. During the preparation phase, CIC members were immersed in the inquiry process through miniprojects, and the results were analyzed. During the pilot projects phase, workshops for teachers, pilot inquiry projects, and planning for a teacher researcher conference took place. The final phase, establishing the infrastructure, focused on developing an institutional program for teaching and supporting collaborative inquiry projects at ISU and for expanded and more sophisticated collaborative inquiry projects at the PDS sites. The paper includes summaries, in table format, of the projects undertaken from spring 1994 through spring 1995. Analysis of the program's progress suggests that: (1) collaborative inquiry appears to flourish more readily in elementary and middle schools than in high schools; (2) more support has been provided for PDS faculty than for ISU faculty; and (3) in general, collaborative inquiry projects became more sophisticated over time. Up to $400 was available to support each collaborative inquiry project. The paper concludes with the call for proposals and the proposal screening criteria.

3.18   Rakow, S. J., & Robinson, L. W. (1997). School and university partnerships: Teaming for success. *Contemporary Education*, 68(2), 143-147.

This article contrasts two PDSs affiliated with University of Houston-Clear Lake. In the first school, becoming a PDS was embraced by a broad segment of teachers; in the second, most teachers viewed the initiative as being relevant only to cooperating teachers. Variables contributing to these diverging responses are discussed, as well as lessons learned.

3.19   Rasch, K., & Finch, M. E. (1996). Who are our partners? Reconceptualizing teaching and stewardship. In T. Warren (Ed.), *Partnerships in teacher education* (pp. 135-142). Lanham, MD: University Press of America.

Chronicled in this chapter are some of the complex relationships and pragmatic successes that have evolved in the teacher education program at Maryville University (MO). The authors focus on an initial block of three preservice courses. Maryville is one of the partners in a local National Network for Educational Renewal site. Through course work and field experiences, the program attempts to foster moral stewardship as a dimension of teaching.

3.20   Reed, C. (1995). *UTEP: The Urban Teacher Education Program. Six-month narrative program report, July 1-December 31, 1994*. Gary: Indiana University Northwest, Urban Teacher Education Program. ED382579

This report discusses progress in achieving goals, general program effectiveness, and progress toward institutionalization of the Urban Teacher Education Program (UTEP) at Indiana University Northwest. The program has two major goals: (1) to change what the urban teacher knows and is able to do and (2) to affect significantly the education of children in the urban school districts of northwest Indiana. UTEP's primary components are: the professional development center (PDC) model for delivery of teacher education and the Option II model for alternative certification of urban teachers. Option II is a graduate certification program that recruits and prepares individuals who already possess an undergraduate degree. The report discusses indicators of program progress in the following areas: policy board and personnel changes, signs of institutionalization, rationale for renewing Option II, urban teacher education curriculum development, professional development activities, program evaluation, student recruitment and support (includes a brief discussion of innovative "compensation" for student teachers), PDC activities, and UTEP outreach. Fourteen attachments, which constitute more than half the report, include summaries of program goals and staff positions and responsibilities, contact information for program staff, Option II renewal rationale statement, revised job descriptions, copies of agendas from various UTEP activities, conference programs, and several news clippings.

3.21   Schack, G., & Overturf, B. J. (1994, April). *Professional development teams: Stepping stone (or next best thing) to professional development schools*. Paper presented at the annual meeting of the American Educational Research Association, New Orleans. ED374090

This paper describes the professional development team (PDT) concept, reports results of a study of the development and year-long implementation of a PDT, and describes the effects of the PDT on school personnel and on subsequent implementation of a professional development school (PDS). The PDT is presented as a viable option for improving K-12 education, research, professional development, and teacher education through school-based interprofessional teams. The PDT that was studied was located in a middle school and consisted of four teachers, one university professor, five student teachers, and two methods field experience students. PDTs have many of the same goals and functions as PDSs; however, PDSs are generally schoolwide efforts rather than efforts that involve only one team of students, teachers, and college faculty. PDTs can serve as a stepping stone to PDS implementation, as well as a viable alternative if a more extensive PDS relationship between a school and a college is not possible. Data sources for the study included surveys of students and parents; participant observation; and interviews with team members, school administrators, and other education professionals. Results indicated that the teachers, students, preservice teachers, and college professor who were associated with the team perceived positive outcomes from the PDT's presence. Among the positive outcomes was the perception by school and college personnel that the PDT's existence laid the foundation for the school's becoming a PDS. Also discussed are some of the negative reactions to the PDT.

3.22   Schneider, H., Seidman, I., & Cannone P. (1994). Ten steps to collaboration: The story of a professional development school. *Teaching and Learning: The Journal of Natural Inquiry*, 8(2), 21-33. EJ492201

This article discusses the development, underlying principles, program objectives, accomplishments, and pitfalls of a school district-university partnership involving University of Massachusetts-Amherst. The partnership established a high school and middle school PDS. Topics include equity among school and university participants, governance, institutionalization, teacher isolation, mentoring, student teacher cohorts, and financing.

3.23 Shen, J. (1994, February). *A study in contrast: Visions of preservice teacher education in the context of a professional development school*. Paper presented at the annual meeting of the American Association of Colleges for Teacher Education, Chicago. ED368677

This study begins with a review of the literature on the professional development school and identifies a conceptual framework underlying the rhetoric for the PDS movement. It then constructs, by employing a case study approach, a school-based PDS faculty's vision of preservice teacher education in the PDS context and the individual and institutional difficulties in realizing their ideal roles. Also contrasted are expectations present in the literature and voices from the field. The practically oriented vision held by the school-based faculty lacked some of the most important ideas expressed in the theoretical conceptual model. Some suggestions are made to improve preservice teacher education in the PDS context. The PDS sampled for this case study was a middle school associated with the Puget Sound Professional Development Center in Washington. Findings from the study indicate that there were three significant differences between the vision of the PDS found in the literature and that revealed by voices from the field. In contrast to the literature, school-based faculty members' visions did not include: (1) the concept of student teacher cohort groups; (2) an awareness that the PDS model is supposed to supply an exemplary setting for student teaching; or (3) the concept of inquiry as part of the PDS mission. The study's findings suggest that successful implementation of the PDS model requires more interaction between school faculty and university faculty to develop a shared vision.

3.24 Snyder, J., Lippincott, A., & Bower, D. (in press). Portfolios in teacher education: Technical or transformational? In N. Lyons (Ed.). *With portfolio in hand: Portfolios in teaching and teacher education*. New York: Teachers College Press.

This chapter addresses the inherent tension that arises from the dual functions of portfolio assessment in teacher education: to support teacher learning and to evaluate qualifications for licensure. Exploring this tension within the context of the masters in education program at University of California-Santa Barbara, the authors conducted a study of two cohorts of student teachers during their professional preparation year and followed a sample of 18 candidates into their first year of teaching. The program requires of candidates two portfolios: the credential portfolio, which addresses state credentialling requirements, and the issue portfolio, which has a student-selected focus. Findings suggest that, overall, the value of the portfolio process is related to the possibilities for reflection constructed over time more than to the portfolio's function or audience.

3.25 Stanulis, R. N. (1995). Classroom teachers as mentors: Possibilities for participation in a professional development school context. *Teaching and Teacher Education, 11*(4), 331-44. EJ525380

A study of five mentors in a K-5 professional development school affiliated with Michigan State University investigated how mentors: (1) talk about their theories of how novices learn to teach; (2) use different sources of knowledge to help novices learn to teach; and (3) model and encourage critical reflection about significant issues in teacher education.

3.26 Stewart, H. (1996). Extended teacher education programs: Collaboration as a tool of implementation. *Journal of Professional Studies, 3*(2), 3-14.

Prospects for PDS implementation in Ontario are considered within the context of recommendations in Ontario's 1994 *Report of the Royal Commission on Learning*. The commission recommended partnering school reform and teacher education reform and highlighted collaboration as the central tool in implementing its recommendations. Responses to the report, and major themes in collaboration, teacher education reform, and implementation challenges and processes are discussed.

3.27 Swanson, J. (1995). *Systemic reform in the professionalism of educators. Volume I: Findings and conclusions. Studies of education reform.* ED397556 (Also available online: http://www.ed.gov/pubs/SER/ProfEd/execsum.html)

Results are reported from in-depth case studies of three school-university partnerships that have undertaken comprehensive reform initiatives focusing on redesign of the teaching and learning process for professional educators. The overall study examines preservice and inservice training and the working conditions of educators. The three sites are the Learning Consortium at the University of Toronto, the Southern Maine Partnership, and the Benedum Project at West Virginia University. Individual case studies, cross-site analysis, and assessment of outcomes are included.

3.28 Teitel, L. (1996). *Professional development schools: A literature review.* Unpublished manuscript. (Available from the Professional Development School Standards Project, National Council for Accreditation of Teacher Education (NCATE), Washington, DC.)

Commissioned by the NCATE Professional Development School Standards Project, this review takes a panoramic look at the PDS literature. Topics included in the discussion are definitions, mission, effectiveness, features, constraints, and problematic issues.

3.29 Teitel, L. (1996) *The transformation of school leadership in professional development schools*. New York: National Center for Restructuring Education, Schools, and Teaching; Teachers College, Columbia University.

Connecting parallel efforts to launch professional development schools and improve the prepration of educational administrators, this paper discusses the development of administrators for learner-center schools. Four sections are included: "Leadership and Professional Development Schools: Critical Pieces of School/University Reform"; "Changing Roles for Teachers and Principals in Professional Development Schools"; "The Preparation and Support of School Leaders in Professional Development Schools"; and "Emerging Themes about Leadership and Learning in Professional Development Schools."

3.30 Teitel, L. (1997). Professional development schools and the transformation of teacher leadership. *Teacher Education Quarterly, 24*(1), 9-22.

New roles and responsibilities, which develop from mission and goals, are being assumed by classroom teachers in PDSs. This paper examines these roles and how teachers are prepared and supported for them. Implications for schools, colleges, and PDS proponents are noted.

3.31 Teitel, L., & DelPrete, T. (1995). *Creating professional development school partnerships. A resource guide.* Boston: Massachusetts Field Center for Teaching and Learning. ED387460

This three-part guide presents information and recommendations from the Massachusetts Professional Development School Network Steering Committee on how to develop a professional development school (PDS) partnership. Part one defines the PDS concept, presents a brief background account of its evolution, and discusses its potential for simultaneously improving teaching and learning through the transformation of school and college structures and practices. Part two identifies five principles and characteristics of PDSs. Comments from teachers, interns, and college faculty involved in PDS partnerships supplement this discussion. Part three offers practical advice, in a question and answer format, on how to form and sustain a PDS. Answers to the following questions are given: (1) Why start a PDS? (2) Who will initiate the partnership? (3) How do schools and colleges find partners? (4) How are partnerships defined and developed? and (5) How do you organize and run a PDS partnership? Concrete examples from within Massachusetts illustrate specific approaches to start-up problems and challenges. This guide includes contact information for members of the Massachusetts Professional Development School Network Steering Committee.

3.32 Teitel, L., Reed, C., & O'Conner, K. (Eds.). (1996). *Institutionalizing professional development schools: Successes, challenges, and continuing tensions.* Unpublished manuscript. National Center for Restructuring Education, Schools, and Teaching; Teachers College, Columbia University, New York.

Five case studies of PDS partnerships in a variety of settings focus on progress toward institutionalizing the PDS model as the "accepted way of doing business" (p. 1). Seven signs of institutionalization are identified, and they form the framework for each study. The concluding essay considers challenges and continuing tensions that sometimes bedevil institutionalization efforts. Among the concerns is that partnerships may be inclined to institutionalize the initiative at a premature stage of development thereby leaving the total PDS mission unfulfilled. This paper is one of five comissioned by the National Center for Restructuring Education, Schools, and Teaching (NCREST) to examine various facets of the PDS movement. anticipated publication date for the collection is fall 1997. [*See also* Berry et al.; Murrell & Borunda.]

3.33   Thacker, D. (1994). Professional development schools (PDS) university student orientation. *Contemporary Education, 65*(4), 224-225. EJ507604

A university liason describes the course work and PDS-based clinical activities for the early field experiences of teacher education students. The author also discusses the roles and duties of school and university faculty who participate in the program.

3.34   Trachtman, R. (1996). *The NCATE professional development school study: A survey of 28 PDS sites.* Unpublished manuscript. (Available from the Professional Development School Standards Project, National Council for Accreditation of Teacher Education, Washington, DC)

This study was comissioned by the Professional Development School Standards Project as part of its effort to identify elements of PDS mission and develop a consensus about good practice in PDS settings. Utilizing reputational sampling techniques, 28 "highly developed" sites were identified and surveyed about their purposes and practices. Findings about these purposes and practices are summarized, examples of common practices are provided, and reported outcomes are discussed.

3.35   Troen, V., & Boles, K. (1994). Two teachers examine the power of teacher leadership. In D. R. Walling (Ed.), *Teachers as leaders. Perspectives on the professional development of teachers* (pp. 275-86), Bloomington, IN: Phi Delta Kappa Educational Foundation.

Teacher leadership in the Learning/Teaching Collaborative emerges naturally from the interests and talents that teachers demonstrate as they engage in alternative professional work. The authors discuss this nontraditional leadership paradigm and activities and effects of its development.

3.36   Tusin, L. F. (1995, February). *Success in the first year of teaching: Effects of a clinical experience program.* Paper presented at the annual meeting of the Association of Teacher Educators, Detroit. ED399216

Findings from a study of seven novice teachers who graduated from Elmhurst College (IL) indicate that the preservice clinical experiences received by these teachers during their participation in the Satellite Program contributed to successful first-year teaching experiences. This follow-up study examines Satellite Program graduates who participated in the program between 1991 and 1993 and who began their first year of teaching in either fall 1992 or fall 1993. Four of the seven beginning teachers were hired by the satellite schools in which they had been placed as student teachers. During interviews, all seven teachers gave credit to their clinical experiences for presenting a realistic perception of schools and teaching. There was evidence that all subjects were able to reflect on their practice, identify strengths and weaknesses, and develop action plans for correction and improvement. Novice teachers discussed a variety of problems encountered during the first year of teaching. For the most part, subjects acknowledged the value of their preservice mentors in providing support and strengthening professional skills. These teachers sought formal and informal mentor relationships during their first year of teaching. The Satellite Program was collaboratively designed by Elmhurst College faculty and faculty from the satellite schools to improve the clinical experience component of the college's teacher education program. Interview questions used in the study are included.

3.37 Valli, L. (1994, April). *Professional development schools: An opportunity to reconceptualize schools and teacher education as empowering learning communities*. Paper presented at the International Seminar on Teacher Education (ISTE) annual meeting, Maastricht, The Netherlands. ED381484

Presented in this paper are personal reflections on the nature of learning and the purpose of schooling and their implications for defining the work of professional development schools. The paper examines the implications of intuitive learning, differences in learning, and political aspects of learning theory for professional development schools. This examination of learning theory suggests that: (1) it is unnecessary to conceptualize totally different types of learning environments for child and adult learners; (2) constructivism offers a powerful theory of child and teacher development; (3) learning should be self-directed, inquiry-oriented, and based on life experience; and (4) learning is both a cultural and a developmental process. Also discussed is a vision of a PDS as an empowering, emancipating learning community that frees people from ignorance and knowledge that is trivial, subjugating, or hegemonic. The paper describes four characteristics of empowering learning communities (constructivist, problem-focused, multicultural and inclusive, and social reconstructionist) and outlines how they can guide PDS work. An example is provided of a learning activity that can be used with both teachers and students and that embodies these characteristics in an integrated fashion. In addition there is a brief discussion of how PDSs as learning communities would differ from traditional schools and teacher preparation. The focus is on textbooks, teacher talk, traditional modes of grouping, and the dominant culture.

3.38   Valli, L., Cooper, D., & Frankes, L. (1997). Professional development schools and equity: A critical analysis of rhetoric and research. In M. W. Apple (Ed.), *Review of research in education 22* (pp. 251-304). Washington, DC: American Educational Research Association.

In reviewing the research literature on professional development schools, the authors attempt to (1) match goals identified by PDS proponents with research-documented changes; (2) determine whether the identified changes represent first- or second-order change; and (3) relate stated PDS goals and reported changes to equity goals. The chapter begins with a definition of PDSs, an explanation of first- and second-order change, and an overview of the concept of equity as articulated in the education literature. The PDS advocacy and research literature are then reviewed within the framework of six themes, and relevant equity implications are discussed.

3.39   Vaughn, A. J. (1996). *School renewal and non-instructional time for teachers: Profiles from the National Network for Educational Renewal.* Reflections on Practice Series No. 1. Seattle: University of Washington, Center for Educational Renewal.

How partner schools within the National Network for Educational Renewal (NNER) have addressed the need to create noninstructional time for educators engaged in school renewal activities is the focus of this monograph. The author outlines basic methods employed by schools nationwide to create noninstructional time. This discussion is followed by profiles of seven partner schools. The profiles describe the school context, approach to providing noninstructional time, and lessons learned from such efforts.

3.40   Warner, A. R. (1996). Funding field-based, technology-intensive professional preparation. *Teacher Education and Practice, 12*(1), 41-46.

This article examines the PDS concept from the perspective of the resources needed to institutionalize field-based, technology-intensive teacher education programs based on the PDS model. The discussion focuses on the needs of the Centers for Professional Development and Technology (CPDTs), funded by the Texas legislature.

3.41   Webb-Dempsey, J. (n.d.). *Benedum Collaborative professional development schools. Impact assessment study. Initial findings from student data collection pilot in the five original PDS sites.* Draft. Unpublished manuscript. West Virginia University, College of Human Resources and Education, Center for the Renewal of Professional Preparation and Practice, Morgantown.

This paper provides an overview of the PDS initiative within the Benedum Collaborative at West Virginia University and discusses the limitations of utilizing traditional measures to assess the impact of PDS programming on students. Selected student performance data are presented, and, overall, the data given reveal positive results in the five original PDS sites. Key lessons that emerged from the study of PDS impact on student experiences are reported within the framework of PDS program belief statements. A more expansive treatment of the impact study's findings can be found in a chapter by the author in a 1997 volume of papers on the Benedum Collaborative. [*See* Hoffman, Reed, & Rosenbluth.]

3.42   Whitford, B. L., & Gaus, D. M. (1995). With a little help from their friends: Teachers making change at Wheeler School. In A. Lieberman (Ed.), *The work of restructuring schools: Building from the ground up* (pp. 18-42). New York: Teachers College Press.

School change, over a six-year period, in an elementary PDS in Jefferson County (KY), is discussed. Changes such as implementing an ungraded program; flexible grouping; teaming; and varied, active learning experiences for children are among the changes noted and described. The authors discuss how these changes came about, what motivated school faculty to try new approaches, and the results of innovations.

3.43   Wiggins, K., Owens, R., & Williams, N. (1994). Attitudes of resident teachers: The DePaul/Glenview teacher prepration program. *Critical Issues in Teacher Education, 4*, 43-51.

Six students who completed a one-year internship and two-year residency were the subjects of the study reported in this article. Data were collected about subjects' perceptions and feelings about how well their educational experiences prepared them for teaching.

3.44   Wiseman, D. L., & Cooner, D. (1996). Discovering the power of collaboration: The impact of a school-university partnership on teaching. *Teacher Education and Practice, 12*(1), 18-28.

This article describes the history, process, and challenges associated with developing a collaboratively designed language arts methods course for preservice students at Texas A & M University. One innovative feature of the course was the writing buddies program, which deployed 100-125 university students to provide one-to-one and small group writing assistance to elementary students. Writing scores on state achievement tests increased from a school pass rate of 69% to 92% after the third year of the writing buddies program. The collaboration also produced professional growth in veteran teachers also and has led to a similar course design at several other schools and experimentation by the original site with the format in a collaboratively taught technology course.

3.45   Woloszyk, C. A., & Davis, S. (1993, February). *Restructuring a teacher preparation program using the professional development school concept.* Paper presented at the annual meeting of the Association of Teacher Educators, Los Angeles. ED360260

Establishing a PDS is a complex process that can be expected to pass through four phases of development: exploration, orientation, implementation, and operation. This paper provides guidelines and identifies issues related to each phase. Two documents are included in the appendices: "Oakland University Michigan and Pontiac Schools Professional Development Schools: Criteria for Partners" and "Application for Oakland University-Pontiac Professional Development School."

3.46   Yopp, H. K., Guillaume, A. M., & Savage, T. V. (1993-1994). Collaboration at the grass roots: Implementing the professional development school concept. *Action in Teacher Education, 5*(4), 29-35.

A successful professional development school project, established by four elementary schools and California State University-Fullerton, has four components: student teacher cohorts, close link between coursework and field experiences, close collaboration between university instructional team and PDS site personnel, and entire staff commitment to student teacher professional development.

Appendix 1

Internet Resources

Listservs

On the PDS-related listservs noted below, subscribers pose and respond to questions from colleagues; announce conferences, new publications, and even job openings; and post full-text documents, which can be accessed and downloaded. To subscribe to any of these listservs, request subscription procedures from each list directly at the e-mail address given below, or request subscription procedures for all lists from the Clinical Schools Clearinghouse (iah@aacte.nche.edu). Topics covered by the first two listservs include all aspects of PDS work while the third focuses on re-search-related topics. The fourth list also focuses on aspects of interprofessional collaboration in partner schools.

PDS-NCREST, sponsored by the National Center for Restructuring Education, Schools, and Teaching, Teachers College, Columbia University
contact: PRL4@COLUMBIA.EDU

PDSnet, sponsored by the Chicago Teachers' Center
contact: uwstack@uxa.ecn.bgu.edu *or*
udsperli@uxa.ecn.bgu.edu

PDS-RES, sponsored by the Johns Hopkins University
contact: especter@jhu.edu

IERLIAIS, sponsored by the Institute for Educational Renewal, Miami University (OH)
contact: yodern@muohio.edu

World Wide Web Sites

The following World Wide Web (WWW) sites and pages provide information on professional development schools and related initiatives. *[Note: URLs current as of June 1997]*

The Clinical Schools Clearinghouse (CSC) maintains a public access site. Information includes: PDS bibliographies, statistics, Internet resources, announcements, sample partnership agreements, and the PDS Database data collection form. The web site provides links to other PDS-related Internet sites and addresses, as well as to full-text ERIC digests on PDS issues.
(http://www.aacte.org/csc/html)

An Annotated Guide to University/School Collaboration in Enhancing Teaching
(http://www.ed.sc.edu/te/42ab.html)

Brandon/Oxford Professional Development School
(http://www.NCREL.ORG/SDRS/AREAS/ISSUES/
ENVRNMNT/GO/94-4BRAN.htm)

Cooperating Teachers Reflect Upon the Impact of
Coaching on Their Own Teaching and Professional Life
(http://olympia.gse.uci.edu/vkiosk/Faculty/aera.html)

Four Cities Urban Professional Development School
Network
(http://www.soe.uwm.edu/soeoffices/4cities.html)

Holmes Partnership
(http://www.udel.edu/holmes/)

Kansas Alliance of Professional Development Schools
(http://www.SOE.UKANS.EDU/SPECIAL_SERVICE/
PDS.html)

Leading Edge PDS Network (Teachers College, Columbia University)
(http://www.tc.columbia.edu/~ncrest/leadedge)

National Center for Restructuring Education, Schools,
and Teaching (NCREST) (Teachers College, Columbia
University)
(http://www.tc.columbia.edu/~ncrest)

The National Commission on Teaching and America's
Future
(http://www.tc.columbia.edu/~teachcomm/)

Professional Development School (John Brown University)
(http://panther.nwsc.k12.ar.us/pds/ppdsind.htm)

Professional Development School (San Diego State
University)
(http://www.cvesd.k12.ca.us/cview/profdeve.htm)

Professional Development Schools in Vermont: Integrating to Improve Learning
(http://ra.terc.edu/hub/regional_networks/k16/pds-
overview.html)

The Regional Alliance Higher Education Reform Network
(http://hub.terc.edu/ra/rns/ed-reform/postings/0423.html)

Scales Professional Development School (Scales
Elementary School/Arizona State University)
(http://seamonkey.ed.asu.edu/~hixson/scales/
scales.html)

Southwestern Washington Regional Collaborative Professional Development Schools
(http://www.educ.wsu.edu/handbook/southwestern.html)

University of California-Irvine
(http://www.gse.usi.edu)

Periodic searches of the WWW, using different search engines, may turn up new Internet resources. In addition, web sites frequently contain links to related Internet resources.

Appendix 2

Newsletters
and
Other Periodicals

Center Correspondent
(Newsletter of the Center for Educational Renewal)
Center for Educational Renewal
Miller Hall DQ-12
University of Washington
Seattle, WA 98195
ph: 206-543-6230

CPDT Network News
(Newsletter of the Texas Centers for Professional Development
and Technology)
CPDT Network
School of Education (EDB 3048)
Southwest Texas State University
601 University Drive
San Marcos, TX 78666
ph: 512-245-2150
fax: 512-245-8345

Four Cities Urban PDS Network!!!
(Newsletter of the Four Cities Urban Professional Development
School Network)
Center for Teacher Education
University of Wisconsin-Milwaukee
P.O. Box 413
Milwaukee, WI 53201
ph: 414-229-5017
fax: 414-229-6548

From the Inside: Perspectives on PDS work
(This is a new education journal focusing on informal practitio-
ner narratives and stories that include concrete, specific descrip-
tions of good practice.)
David Leo-Nyquist, Editor
From the Inside
Box 247
Saint Michael's College
Winooski Park

Colchester, VT 05439
ph: 802-654-2279
fax: 802-654-2610

Institute for Educational Renewal Newsletter
IER
203 McGuffey Hall
Miami University
Oxford, OH 45056
ph: 513-529-6926

PDS Collaborator
(Newsletter of the PDS program of Indiana State University)
School of Education
Indiana State University
Terre Haute, IN 47809
ph: 812-237-2846

PDS Happenings
(Newsletter of Thompson Valley High School, Colorado State
University partner school)
Imo Jeane Mayes
PDS Coordinator
Thompson Valley High School
1669 Eagle Drive
Loveland, CO 80537
ph: 970-669-0801, Ext. 128

PDS Network News
(Newsletter of the NCREST PDS Network)
NCREST - Box 110
Teachers College, Columbia University
New York, NY 10027
ph: 212-678-4196
fax: 212-678-4170

PDS News Notes
(Newsletter of the Teachers College PDS Project)
Professional Development School Project
Box 155, Teachers College
Columbia University
525 West 120th Street
New York, NY 10027
ph: 212-678-3166 or 3477
fax: 212-678-4710

PDS Proceedings
(Newsletter of the University of South Carolina Professional
Development Schools Network)
PDS Network
102 Wardlaw
University of South Carolina
Columbia, SC 29208
ph: 803-777-3828

Appendix 3

Videos

American Association of Colleges for Teacher Education (AACTE). (1994). *Teachers for Tomorrow. A symposium. Outcomes and implications of a clinical schools demonstration project.* (120 min.). Washington, DC: Author. ($25, available: AACTE Publications, One Dupont Circle, NW, Suite 610, Washington, DC 20036; 202-293-2450)

   This videotape features 25 teachers, principals, teacher education students, and university faculty members from the five Teachers for Tomorrow sites in a reflective conversation about their experiences as participants in a 3-year effort to establish and expand urban PDS partnerships. The videotape was filmed at the 1994 AACTE annual meeting and includes exchanges among the program participants and prominent educators, as well as audience questions.

Century Communications. (1996). *The Students as Authors project. Education showcase: Cover story.* (120 min.). Morgantown, WV: Author. (available: Central Elementary School, Morgantown, WV)

   The *Students as Authors* project is a literacy development program based at an elementary PDS, which participates in the Benedum Collaborative affiliated with West Virginia University.

National Center for Restructuring Education, Schools, and Teaching (NCREST). (1995). *Preparing teachers for learner centered practice: The professional development school at PS 87.* (17 min.) New York: National Center for Restructuring Education, Schools, and Teaching; Teachers College, Columbia University, New York. ($19.95, available: NCREST, Box 117, Teachers College, Columbia University, New York, NY 10027; 212-678-3432)

   A new kind of collaboration for preservice teacher preparation and inservice professional development is demonstrated in this documentary about the partnership between Teachers College, Columbia University, and a New York City elementary school.

National Center for Restructuring Education, Schools, and Teaching, (NCREST). (1996). *The lightning post-office.* (20 min.) New York: National Center for Restructuring Education, Schools, and Teaching; Teachers College, Columbia University. ($19.95, available: NCREST, Box 117, Teachers College, Columbia University, New York, NY 10027; 202-678-3432)

   At PS 87 in NYC, first graders create a school-wide post office—transforming their research about their neighborhood post office into a real-life work place. Students use skills from a variety of disciplines as they organize and design the project, discuss and solve problems related to their jobs, and explore their school environment.

National Commission on Teaching and America's Future. (1996). ***What matters most: Teaching for America's future*** (30 min.). New York: Author. ($15, available from: The National Commission on Teaching & America's Future, Teachers College, Columbia University, Box 117, 525 West 120th Street, New York, NY 10027; 212-678-3204)

Among the recommendations of the National Commission on Teaching and America's Future are a number of proposals to improve teaching throughout the professional career. This video illustrates the major points of the Commission's report with vignettes on these subjects: (1) new models for teacher preparation; (2) support for beginning teachers; (3) rewards for teaching knowledge and skill; (4) redesigning professional development; and (5) restructuring schools.

University of North Florida, College of Education and Human Services. (1995). ***First Coast Urban Academy for Excellence in Teaching***. Jacksonville, FL: Author. (4-tape package $130, available from: First Coast Urban Academy for Excellence in Teaching, Office of Sponsored Research and Training, University of North Florida, College of Education and Human Services, 4567 St. Johns Bluff Road South, Jacksonville, FL 32224-2645). ED401224

This package contains four videotapes: "Process-Oriented Learning" (27 minutes); "Developing Cooperative Citizens" (23 minutes); "Culturally Sensitive Learning" (27 minutes); and "Technologically Competent Learning" (16 minutes). The videotapes are accompanied by a 23-page manual, "Guidelines for the Use of Video Episodes." This material presents some of the outcomes of the First Coast Urban Academy for Excellence in Teaching, a professional development model designed to promote the professional growth of teachers in urban settings and the implementation of Florida Blueprint 2000. The academy was collaboratively developed by University of North Florida, Duval County Public Schools, and Duval Teachers United.

Appendix 4

Networks and Information Centers

Centers for Professional Development & Technology (CPDT)
Education Preparation
Texas Education Agency
1701 North Congress
Austin, TX 78701
512-305-8701
>The statewide network of CPDTs includes several partnerships, which are partially funded by state funds. A number of these partnerships publish newsletters.

Clinical Schools Clearinghouse
AACTE
One Dupont Circle NW, Suite 610
Washington, DC 20036
202-293-2450
e-mail: iah@aacte.nche.edu
>The clearinghouse collects and abstracts PDS literature for the ERIC database; disseminates information on PDSs; schedules workshops; conducts surveys; publishes bibliographies, directories, digests, and other material related to PDSs; and publishes the *Clinical Schools Update*, a periodic insert, which appears in the AACTE newsletter, *Briefs*.

Four Cities Urban PDS Network
Center for Teacher Education
University of Wisconsin-Milwaukee
P.O. Box 413
Milwaukee, WI 53201
414-229-5017
e-mail: aotis@soe.uwm.edu
>The Four Cities Network includes University of Wisconsin-Milwaukee, University of Chicago-Chicago Circle, Roosevelt University, University of Detroit-Mercy, and Cleveland State University.

The Holmes Partnership
Office of the Dean
College of Education
The Ohio State University
127 Arps Hall
1945 North High Street
Columbus, OH 43210
614-292-2461

This organization evolved from the Holmes Group, whose design principles for professional development schools have shaped PDS development for the last decade. Members of the new organization will include local school-university PDS partnerships and national organizations.

Massachusetts Field Center for Teaching and Learning
University of Massachusetts Boston
100 Morrisey Blvd.
Boston, MA 02125
617-287-7660
The center, the base for a statewide network of school and university educators, serves as a resource for practitioners by collecting and sharing information on new and innovative programs and materials. It's newsletter, *Teaching Voices*, features teacher work, as well as announcements of workshops, grants, and conferences.

National Center for Restructuring Education, Schools, and Teaching (NCREST)
Teachers College, Box 110
Columbia University
New York, NY 10027
212-678-3763
e-mail: PRL4@Columbia.edu
NCREST sponsors the PDS Network, an association of institutions involved in PDS activities. The group publishes a newsletter, *PDS Network News*; manages a listserv; sponsors conferences; and has produced videos on PDSs.

National Network for Educational Renewal (NNER)
Center for Educational Renewal (CER)
College of Education
University of Washington
313 Miller Hall Box 353600
Seattle, WA 98195-3600
206-543-6230
Sixteen NNER partnerships have established more than 300 partner schools in 14 states; the 19 Goodlad postulates guide the design of these programs. *Center Correspondent* is a newsletter published by CER.

Professional Development Schools Standards Project
National Council for Accreditation of Teacher Education (NCATE)
2010 Massachusetts Avenue NW, Suite 500
Washington, DC 20036-1023
202-466-7496
    The PDS Standards Project is a 2-year project, begun in 1995, which has conducted a number of inquiry activities designed to inform the project's primary task—the construction of draft developmental standards for PDSs.

St. Louis Professional Development Schools Collaborative (PDSC)
Dr. Wayne Walker, Coordinator
St. Louis Public Schools
1110 Victor St.
St. Louis, MO 63104
(314) 771-6382
    The PDSC includes eight higher education institutions and 18 school-university partnerships. Eight school districts and two private schools are represented.

Appendix 5

Clinical Schools Clearinghouse
and Adjunct ERIC Clearinghouse on Clinical Schools

PURPOSE

■ Provides a source of information on professional development schools (PDSs), clinical schools, partner schools, professional practice schools, and similar institutions

■ Acquires, abstracts, and processes literature on professional development schools for the ERIC database

■ Produces bibliographies, periodic papers, digests, and other material on PDS issues

■ Collects data on PDSs

CALL FOR LITERATURE

The Clinical Schools Clearinghouse (CSC) actively seeks literature on topics related to clinical schools, professional development schools, or professional practice schools. The clearinghouse facilitates dissemination of this material via the ERIC database and CSC publications. CSC welcomes:

■ Research Reports
■ Course Descriptions
■ Project Descriptions
■ Curriculum Guides
■ Conference Papers
■ Practice-oriented Materials
■ Literature Reviews
■ State Laws and Regulations
■ Journal Articles
■ Bibliographies
■ Partnership Agreements
■ Handbooks and Directories
■ Audiovisual Material
■ Other Related Information
■ Teacher-produced Material
■ Internet & World Wide Web Sources

PDS Database

The Clinical Schools Clearinghouse (CSC) maintains a searchable database, which contains information on more than 350 K-12 professional development schools and over 80 partnerships. Records include data on, program features, funding, network affiliation, and partners, as well as contact information. To contribute information on your PDS sites and partnership or to obtain information from the database, contact CSC.

TO SUBMIT DOCUMENTS OR OBTAIN MORE INFORMATION, CONTACT:

Ismat Abdal-Haqq, Coordinator
Adjunct ERIC Clearinghouse on Clinical Schools
American Association of Colleges for Teacher Education
One Dupont Circle NW, Suite 610
Washington, DC 20036
ph: 202-293-2450; 1-800-822-9229
fax: 202-457-8095
e-mail: iabdalha@inet.ed.gov *or* iah@aacte.nche.edu
URL: http://www.aacte.org/menu2.html

PDS Publications
from
American Association of Colleges for Teacher Education
ERIC Clearinghouse on Teaching and Teacher Education
Adjunct ERIC Clearinghouse on Clinical Schools

Professional Development Schools: Weighing the Evidence.
Ismat Abdal-Haqq. Winter 1997. Contact Corwin Press for price
& ordering information: phone 805-499-9774; e-mail: order
@corwin.sagepub.com.

Reviews recent literature related to the four major PDS
goals—initial teacher preparation, inservice professional development, student learning, and applied inquiry. Topics include
program features, evaluation and outcomes, PDS interface with
three reform initiatives—integrated services, technology infusion, and parent involvement—equity, time, and, financing. The
review illuminates what actually goes on in PDSs, how programs deal with thorny issues, the extent to which existing
programs fulfill the PDS mission, and the model's potential for
bringing about meaningful improvements in schooling, particularly for marginalized and vulnerable groups.

*Professional Development Schools: Policy and Financing. A
Guide for Policymakers.* Richard W. Clark. 1997. $7

This booklet provides practical guidelines, with model
financing plans, for policymakers, K-16 faculty, and administrators involved in policy and practice in professional development
schools.

*Professional Development Schools: A Directory of Projects in
the United States.* Second Edition. Ismat Abdal-Haqq. 1995.
$18

Includes: Expanded, updated edition of the 1992 professional development schools (PDSs) directory published by the
Adjunct ERIC Clearinghouse on Clinical Schools; profiles of
more than 300 P-12 PDS sites and over 65 partnerships; information on 50 higher education institutions and 175 PDSs not
included in the previous edition; findings from the second
national PDS survey—contact information and program features, including: partners; funding; affiliations; computer technology; faculty involvement; college-school cooperation;

multicultural issues; grade level; preservice inservice and beginning teacher programs.

Professional Development Schools: A Directory of Projects in the United States. Ismat Abdal-Haqq.1992. $15 (AACTE members)/ $18 (nonmembers)

This directory contains information on more than 125 professional development schools, professional practice schools, and clinical schools. Data are reported from a national survey of professional development schools: collaborative partners and activities; preservice, beginning, & inservice teachers programs; multicultural issues; funding sources; network or consortium affiliations; address, grade level, site coordinators, starting date.

Buy both editions of *Professional Development Schools: A Directory of Projects in the United States* and save. $25 (AACTE members)/$29 (nonmembers)

Professional Development Schools: Toward a New Relationship for Schools and Universities, Trends and Issues Paper No. 3. Raphael O. Nystrand. 1991. $6

This paper traces the development of the PDS concept and discusses issues related to establishing PDSs. Topics include PDS goals, characteristics, and rationale.

Voices of Change: A Report of the Clinical Schools Project, C. Raymond Anderson, Ed. 1992. $17

This monograph reports observations, experiences, and outcomes from the seven clinical sites that participated in the Ford Foundation Clinical Schools Project.

Teachers for Tomorrow. A Symposium: Outcomes & Implications of a Clinical Schools Demonstration Project. 1994. Video: 120 minutes. $25

Teams of teacher education students and school & college faculty from the five urban sites of the AT&T Teachers for Tomorrow program engage in a reflective conversation about the features, activities, and outcomes of this 3-year demonstration project. Topics include recruitment & retention of teachers for urban schools, institutionalization, portfolio assessment, school & college faculty roles, & student teacher cohorts.

FREE PUBLICATIONS

Professional Development School Projects, Mini-Bibliography No. 1. 1991.

Collaboration Within the Context of Professional Development Schools, Mini-Bibliography No. 2. 1991.

Professional Development Schools: Principles and Concepts, Mini-Bibliography No. 3. 1991.

Teacher Education and Professional Development Schools, Mini-Bibliography No. 4. 1992.

Professional Development Schools and Educational Reform: Concepts and Concerns, ERIC Digest 91-2. 1991.

Professionalizing Teaching: Is There a Role for Professional Development Schools? ERIC Digest 91-3. 1992.

Locating Resources on Professional Development Schools, ERIC Digest 95-3. 1996.

TO ORDER

Contact: AACTE, Publications Department, One Dupont Circle NW, Suite 610, Washington, DC 20036-1186, (202) 293-2450, nnc@aacte.nche.edu.

For free publications, contact the Clinical Schools Clearinghouse, One Dupont Circle NW, Suite 610, Washington, DC 20036-1186, (202) 293-2450 or 1-800-822-9229, iah@aacte.nche.edu.